HEALTHY HOMEMADE DOG FOOD COOKBOOK & GUIDE

TRANSFORM YOUR DOG'S LIFE AND DISCOVER HEALTHY, NATURAL, NUTRITIOUS, EASY-TO-MAKE RECIPES

HELEN SUTHERLAND

Copyright © 2023 by Helen Sutherland

All rights reserved.

No part of this book may be reproduced in any form or by any electronic or mechanical means, including information storage and retrieval systems, without written permission from the author, except for the use of brief quotations in a book review.

The content contained within this book may not be reproduced, duplicated or transmitted without direct written permission from the author or the publisher.

Under no circumstances will any blame or legal responsibility be held against the publisher, or author, for any damages, reparation, or monetary loss due to the information contained within this book. Either directly or indirectly. You are responsible for your own choices, actions, and results.

Legal Notice:

This book is copyright protected. This book is only for personal use. You cannot amend, distribute, sell, use, quote or paraphrase any part, or the content within this book, without the consent of the author or publisher.

Disclaimer Notice:

Please note the information contained within this document is for educational and entertainment purposes only. All effort has been executed to present accurate, up to date, and reliable, complete information. No warranties of any kind are declared or implied. Readers acknowledge that the author is not engaging in the rendering of legal, financial, medical or professional advice. The content within this book has been derived from various sources. Please consult a licensed professional before attempting any techniques outlined in this book.

By reading this document, the reader agrees that under no circumstances is the author responsible for any losses, direct or indirect, which are incurred as a result of the use of the information contained within this document, including, but not limited to, errors, omissions, or inaccuracies.

© Copyright Twenty Dogs Publishing/Helen Sutherland 2023 - All rights reserved.

CONTENTS

1. INTRODUCTION	1
Butchers Best Banquet	5
2. DOG DIGESTION	8
The Basics of Dog Digestion	8
3. BARF, PMR AND THE DIY DIET	13
Biologically Appropriate Raw Food (BARF) Diet	14
Prey Model Raw (PMR) Diet	14
Do-It-Yourself (DIY) Diet	15
4. PROTEINS, CARBS AND VITAMINS	16
5. 7 DAY MENU FOR A MONTH OF DAILY MEALS	21
7 meals for a month	27
Beefy Green Cottage Delight	30
Chicken & Veggie Power Bowl	31
Butchers Bonanza	32
Savory Salmon Medley	34
Turkey Superfood Scramble	35
Lamb & Quinoa Goodness	36
Salmon and Sweet Potato Mash	37
6. SINGLE MEAL ADULT DOG RECIPES	39
Turkey and Quinoa Bowl	39
Beef and Chickpea Stew	40
Lentil and Veggie Mix	40
Egg and Spinach Scramble	41
Fish and Green Pea Medley	41
Turkey and Pumpkin Stew	42
Duck and Green Bean Bowl	42
Turkey and Quinoa Bowl	43
7. RECIPES FOR COMMON CONDITIONS	44
Protein Allergies	44
Food Sensitivities	45
Chicken and Sweet Potato Mash	48

Grain-Free Salmon and Vegetable Medley	48
Beef and Chickpea Stew	49
Lentil and Veggie Mix	49
Egg and Spinach Scramble	50
Fish and Green Pea Medley	50
Turkey and Pumpkin Stew	51
Duck and Green Bean Bowl	51
Weight Management	52
Lean Turkey and Vegetable Stew	52
Salmon and Quinoa Salad	54
Chicken and Green Bean Stir-Fry	55
Turkey Meatball Soup	57
Vegetable and Lentil Stew	58
Digestive Disorders	59
Sensitive Stomach Pork and Vegetable Stir-Fry	60
Turkey and Rice Delight	62
Salmon and Sweet Potato Medley	63
Beef and Vegetable Stew	64
Fish and Sweet Potato Mash	65
Urinary Tract Health	66
Chicken and Quinoa Delight	67
Salmon and Sweet Potato Stew	68
Turkey and Cranberry Delight	69
Beef and Barley Stew	70
Tuna and Chickpea Salad	71
Skin and Coat Issues	72
Dental Health:	72
Joint Health:	72
Chicken and Oatmeal with Blueberries	74
Sardine and Sweet Potato Mash	74
Turkey, Quinoa, and Spinach Bowl	75
Beef and Chickpea Stew with Pumpkin	75
Salmon and Lentil Medley	76
Tofu and Sweet Potato Bowl	76
Lamb and Barley with Carrots	77
Pork and Brown Rice with Green Beans	77
Egg, Cottage Cheese, and Raspberry Scramble	78
Venison, Sweet Potato, and Turmeric Mash	78

8. PUPPY RECIPES	79
Vitamins for puppies	81
Chicken and Sweet Potato Mash	85
Beef and Rice Delight	86
Salmon and Quinoa Delight	87
Turkey and Brown Rice Bowl	88
Lamb and Vegetable Stew	89
Tuna and Chickpea Salad	90
Pork and Pumpkin Mash	91
Chicken Liver and Carrot Stir-Fry	92
Duck and Green Bean Medley	93
Quinoa and Black Bean Fiesta	94
9. RECIPES FOR SENIOR DOGS	95
Vitamins and minerals	97
Chicken and Brown Rice Medley	100
Turkey and Sweet Potato Stew	101
Salmon and Quinoa Delight	102
Beef and Vegetable Stir-Fry	103
Lamb and Sweet Potato Casserole	104
Chicken Liver and Quinoa Pilaf	105
Turkey and Vegetable Stew	106
Fish and Potato Bake	107
Pork and Vegetable Stir-Fry	108
Lamb and Lentil Stew	109
10. DOG TREAT RECIPES	110
Liver Cake	110
Peanut Butter Banana Bites	112
Carrot and Apple Biscuits	113
Sweet Potato Chews	114
Blueberry and Yogurt Frozen Treats	115
Salmon and Sweet Potato Balls	116
Spinach and Cheese Biscuits	117
Pumpkin and Oatmeal Cookies	118
Apple and Cinnamon Biscuits	119
Carrot and Apple Biscuits	120

11. FOODS TO AVOID   121
    Foods to avoid   121
    Other foods that can cause problems   123

12. CONCLUSION   126

13. FOOD PROTEINS AND CALORIC SUMMARY   129
    Meat   129
    Fish   130

14. MEASURING VITAMINS AND MINERALS   131
    Measurements and amounts   131

15. VITAMINS AND MINERALS DIARY   137
    Meat, fish and poultry   137
    Dairy   139
    Vegetables and fruits   140
    Legumes   142
    Grains   143

16. SHOPPING LIST   144

17. MORE INFORMATION   147

    Recommended Dog Training Course   149
    More books from Twenty Dogs Publishing   151
    Leave a Review   155

CHAPTER 1
INTRODUCTION

started my journey into making my own dog food after one of my dogs, Millie, began suffering from skin allergies that got worse as she got older. I was using grain-free then discovered that I had to be careful with only feeding grain-free. It lead me down a path of looking closely at dog food ingredients and thinking back to my great grandfather.

He was a dog breeder and dog trainer and he always believed that dogs should eat what we eat (these were the days before fast food restaurants and so on!).

My 'other' job is writing about health and nutrition in humans and I avoided dogs for a long time because I am not a vet and I know that a dogs system is not the same as ours but, I discovered, there are many similarities in terms of vitamins, hormones and what our body systems do. I believe we really are what we eat and so it just made sense that the diet I provide my own dogs needed work on my part and that it was worth sharing.

If we know what a dog needs and what his daily requirements are, then we at least have the tools and the knowledge to know what to cook for our dogs or to know what to look out for in shop bought food. It means that I do provide a bit of detail, but I hope that the recipes are easy to follow.

My first foray was dog treats - specifically liver cake. It was (and is) one of the best puppy training devices I have ever known! I won't cover making your own dog treats in depth but I have included some recipes - including my own Liver Cake Recipe. If you have a puppy, then this is a must!

After making treats, I eventually started using a local butcher who provided me with ground meat that he had left over and from there I began making my own dog food. Since then, (along with the help of coconut oil) Millie's skin is much better and she no longer uses any medicated shampoo or needs steroids. What surprised me most was that it was a lot less expensive than the food I was buying and it took a lot less time than I had imagined.

As you know, when it comes to feeding our furry friends, it's important to provide a balanced diet, and just like us humans, different dog breeds have different nutritional needs. Factors like age, activity level, and overall health also play a role. So, let's dig into what's essential for everyday dog and puppy nutrition that we cover in the following pages.

First up, proteins. Dogs are carnivores at heart, which means their bodies thrive on protein. Think of it as the building block for their muscles, organs, and overall well-being. High-quality animal-based proteins like chicken, beef, turkey, and fish provide essential amino acids to keep your dog in tip-top shape.

INTRODUCTION 3

Next, we've got fats. Good fats are essential for our dogs. They provide energy, promote healthy skin and coat, and help with vitamin absorption. Healthy fats include omega-3 and omega-6 fatty acids, which can be found in fish oil, flaxseed oil, and some plant oils.

Carbohydrates are another part of the canine nutrition equation. While dogs don't need carbs in the same way we do, they can still benefit from the energy and nutrients they provide. Plus, carbs can be great for dogs with food sensitivities or allergies. Think sweet potatoes, peas, or brown rice.

Now, let's not forget vitamins and minerals. We cover these all in more detail in a Chapter 4. These micronutrients are crucial for various bodily functions, such as growth, immune system support, and bone health. Some of the key players are:

- Vitamin A for vision, growth, and a healthy immune system
- B vitamins for energy, metabolism, and nervous system function
- Vitamin C for immune support and as an antioxidant
- Vitamin D for bone and muscle health
- Calcium and phosphorus for strong bones and teeth
- Iron for oxygen transportation in the bloodstream

So, how do we make sure our dogs get all these essential nutrients? By including a variety of ingredients like lean meats, fish, eggs, fruits, veggies, and healthy oils, you can provide balanced nutrition for your pup.

For instance, the recipe with chicken, brown rice, and veggies is a protein-packed meal with wholesome carbs and essential nutrients. Chicken provides a great source of protein and brown rice offers a complex carb that is gentle on your dog's stomach. The mixed veggies contribute vitamins and minerals to keep your dog healthy and happy.

Another example, the salmon and quinoa recipe, it is fantastic for dogs with food sensitivities or allergies. Salmon is a protein source rich in omega-3 fatty acids, supporting your dog's skin, coat, and immune system. Quinoa, a gluten-free carb, provides energy and fiber, while the veggies add vitamins and minerals for overall health.

I called my first efforts Butchers Banquet and I use ground up meat from the butcher that is made from the end cuts of meat. Not only is it very cost effective but by using end cuts, I am making sure that no part of the animal goes to waste.

However, end cuts can sometimes be higher in fat, which may not be ideal for dogs prone to obesity or those with specific dietary restrictions. So be sure to ask your butcher about the fat content of the meat, as well as its overall content, and trim any excess fat if necessary.

To turn that ground butcher's meat into a well-rounded meal I added a mix of carbohydrates, vegetables, and some ingredients for those essential nutrients. Here's my simple recipe to get you started.

INTRODUCTION

BUTCHERS BEST BANQUET

Ingredients:

- 2 pound ground butcher's meat (beef, chicken, turkey, or lamb)
- 2 cup cooked brown rice or quinoa (I often add sweet potato's as well)
- 2 cup mixed vegetables (like peas, carrots, or green beans), cooked and chopped
- 1/2 cup cooked, chopped leafy greens (like spinach or kale)
- 1 tablespoon ground flaxseed (for omega-3 fatty acids)
- 1 teaspoon calcium supplement (powdered form, as recommended by your vet)

Instructions:

1. Cook the ground meat in a skillet (I also use a plain old pot) over medium heat until browned and cooked through. Drain any excess fat if needed.
2. In a large bowl, combine the cooked meat, cooked rice or quinoa, cooked mixed vegetables, and leafy greens. I sometimes add raw carrots for extra 'bite'
3. Mix in the ground flaxseed and/or calcium supplement until well combined.
4. Let the mixture cool before serving it to your dog. You can refrigerate any leftovers in an airtight container for up to 3 days or pop in the freezer.

I like my herbal remedies so I can't resist adding turmeric. I often add a quarter to half a teaspoon per 2lbs of meat. Turmeric contains a compound called curcumin, which has anti-inflammatory, antioxidant, and potential anti-cancer properties. These benefits can help support your dog's joint health, boost their immune system, and improve their overall wellbeing.

To include turmeric in the recipe I provided earlier, you can follow these guidelines:

1. Start with a small amount: For a dog of average size, begin with 1/8 to 1/4 teaspoon of turmeric powder per day, mixed into their food. You can gradually increase the amount to around 1/2 teaspoon per day, based on your dog's size and tolerance.
2. Combine with black pepper: Adding a pinch of black pepper can enhance the absorption of curcumin in your dog's body. Black pepper contains a compound called piperine, which can increase the bioavailability of curcumin by up to 2000%. (This is true for humans as well).
3. Mix with a healthy fat: Curcumin is fat-soluble, so combining it with a healthy fat, such as the ground flaxseed already in the recipe, can improve absorption.

To prepare multiple meals at once, you can easily scale up the recipe by doubling or tripling the ingredient amounts, then portioning and storing the prepared food in the refrigerator or freezer.

I love this recipe as do my dogs. It's very easy to make and I tend to batch up and store in the freezer.

As you might guess, I am a fan of the DIY diet and I briefly cover the different types of diet in the next chapter. I am not convinced

INTRODUCTION

there is too much difference between BARF, PMR or DIY other than the ease of preparation, cost and sourcing. Whatever you decide, the key is to create a balanced meal plan that meets your dog's specific needs.

By combining different recipes that offer complementary nutrients, you'll ensure that your dog gets a complete and varied diet. In the 7 day 30 day plan chapter I show the what each meal delivers in terms of daily requirements. I don't show this all the time but I think it helps to get us thinking about what we are providing for our pups.

Just bear in mind that canine nutrition can vary based on breed, age, activity level, and overall health. A balanced diet consisting of proteins, fats, carbs, vitamins, and minerals is essential for your dog's well-being. By creating homemade meals using the recipes provided, you can support your dog's health and happiness. I will say this more than once, but please be sure you consult with your vet before making any changes to your dog's diet.

Happy cooking and tail-wagging!

CHAPTER 2
DOG DIGESTION

THE BASICS OF DOG DIGESTION

Dogs are omnivores, meaning they can eat both plant and animal-based foods. Their digestive system is designed to break down and absorb a variety of nutrients, including carbohydrates, proteins, and fats.

The Importance of a Balanced and Nutritious Diet for Dogs

It's essential to ensure that your dog is getting a balanced and nutritious diet that meets their needs. A balanced diet for dogs should include a variety of proteins, carbohydrates, and fats, as well as essential vitamins and minerals. Grains such as corn, wheat, and rice are an important source of carbohydrates for dogs and provide essential energy for their daily activities.

It means that their food should include high-quality proteins, carbohydrates, and fats, as well as essential vitamins and minerals as well as one that is appropriate for your dog's age, weight, and activity level (which is why you will see puppy, adult and senior varieties in the store).

One popular trend in dog food is grain-free diets, but they may not always be the best choice for every dog. I take a look at this in a later chapter and provide some homemade grain free recipes that mean that your dog should still be getting the vitamins and minerals that he needs.

Int his chapter I wanted to summaries the main body systems of your dog. Like us, the body systems are complex and they all work together like a well-oiled machine to maintain overall health and well-being.

A dog's body systems include the digestive system, respiratory system, circulatory system, nervous system, musculoskeletal system, and endocrine system, among others. Understanding how these systems work and what hormones, vitamins, and minerals help support each one is not essential but it can help to have some knowledge of them. You may never hear about a dogs hormone health for example, but like humans, you might one day soon! I don't cover hormones in this book but I wanted to mention them because I believe they are just as important to our dogs as they are to all of us.

Digestive System

The digestive system of a dog is responsible for breaking down food, absorbing nutrients, and eliminating waste. The system includes the mouth, teeth, esophagus, stomach, small intestine, large intestine, and rectum. Hormones that support the digestive system include gastrin, secretin, and cholecystokinin, which stimulate the production of digestive juices and control the rate at which food moves through the digestive tract.

Vitamins and minerals that support the digestive system include Vitamin B12, which helps in the production of red blood cells, and iron, which is important for the formation of hemoglobin, a protein that carries oxygen in the blood.

Respiratory System

The respiratory system of a dog is responsible for exchanging oxygen and carbon dioxide, and includes the nose, pharynx, larynx, trachea, bronchi, and lungs. Hormones that support the respiratory system include epinephrine, which increases the heart rate and breathing rate, and cortisol, which helps the body respond to stress.

Vitamins and minerals that support the respiratory system include Vitamin C, which helps maintain the health of the respiratory tract, and magnesium, which helps relax the muscles in the airways.

Circulatory System

The circulatory system of a dog is responsible for carrying blood, oxygen, and nutrients to the body's cells and removing waste products. The system includes the heart, blood vessels, and blood. Hormones that support the circulatory system include adrenaline, which increases heart rate and blood pressure, and antidiuretic hormone, which regulates fluid balance.

Vitamins and minerals that support the circulatory system include Vitamin K, which helps blood to clot, and potassium, which helps regulate heart function.

Nervous System

The nervous system of a dog is responsible for transmitting messages throughout the body and controlling the body's functions. The system includes the brain, spinal cord, and nerves. Hormones that support the nervous system include dopamine, which helps regulate mood, and serotonin, which helps regulate sleep and appetite. Vitamins and minerals that support the nervous system include Vitamin B6, which helps in the production of neurotransmitters, and calcium, which is important for proper nerve function.

Musculoskeletal System

The musculoskeletal system of a dog is responsible for movement and support, and includes the bones, muscles, tendons, and ligaments. Hormones that support the musculoskeletal system include growth hormone, which promotes bone growth, and testosterone (which promotes muscle growth). Vitamins and minerals that support the musculoskeletal system include Vitamin D, which helps the body absorb calcium, and magnesium, which helps muscles to contract and relax.

Endocrine System

The endocrine system of a dog is responsible for producing and releasing hormones, which regulate the body's functions. The

12   HEALTHY HOMEMADE DOG FOOD COOKBOOK & GUIDE

system includes the adrenal glands, pancreas, thyroid, and pituitary gland.

Hormones that support the endocrine system include insulin, which regulates blood sugar levels, and thyroid hormones, which regulate metabolism. Vitamins and minerals that support the endocrine system include Vitamin B complex, which helps in the production of hormones, and selenium, which

Now its time to work towards our recipes but first of all let's take a brief look at the different diets and dog foods.

CHAPTER 3
BARF, PMR AND THE DIY DIET

There really isn't anything badly wrong with most packaged dog foods, either wet or dry, as long as you know what is in them and that they have the vitamins and nutrients that your dog needs.

But, and there is a but, by necessity they contain additives that are needed to either preserve or color them, and some have too much water (some wet foods), or fat content or limited essential vitamins, and some even have very little meat content.

I don't want decry all packaged or pre-made dog food as it would do a disservice to the many people who work very hard to deliver nutritious food in a packaged and lasting form. I prefer not to use it, but I do use it sometimes. It's simply a personal choice.

I feel this way about the Biologically Appropriate Raw Food (BARF) and Prey Model Raw (PMR) diets too. As long as the essential vitamins and minerals are there, and you have the time, that too is a personal choice because if your dog is getting what it needs to be healthy then there can't be a difference to overall health. Let's take a quick look at these diets for those of you who want to know what they mean.

BIOLOGICALLY APPROPRIATE RAW FOOD (BARF) DIET

The BARF diet emphasizes feeding raw, unprocessed food to dogs, including meat, bones, fruits, vegetables, and some dairy.

Advocates claim that the BARF diet more closely resembles a dog's natural diet and provides better nutrition, leading to shinier coats, healthier skin, improved energy levels, and reduced stool volume and odor.

PREY MODEL RAW (PMR) DIET

The PMR diet focuses on feeding dogs raw, whole-animal carcasses or a combination of raw meat, organs, and bones, to mimic the consumption of prey in the wild.

PMR proponents believe this diet promotes optimal health by more closely resembling a dog's natural diet, leading to benefits similar to those of the BARF diet (coat, skin, energy, and reduced stool volume and odor).

Like the BARF diet, potential risks include bacterial contamination, nutritional imbalances, and injury from bone fragments.

PMR diets tend to be more costly and time-consuming because its more difficult to source and prepare.

DO-IT-YOURSELF (DIY) DIET

DIY diets involve dog owners creating homemade meals for their pets, which can include raw or cooked ingredients.

As with any diet, the main challenge with DIY diets is creating a balanced and nutritionally complete meal plan. There's a risk of nutritional deficiencies or imbalances if the you don't have an understanding of your dogs nutritional requirements.

DIY diets, like BARF or PMR mean that you can tailor recipes to meet your dog's specific needs or preferences and eliminate artificial additives, preservatives, or low-quality ingredients.

So what are these vitamins and minerals. I cover this in the next chapter before we move on to the menu's and recipes!

CHAPTER 4
PROTEINS, CARBS AND VITAMINS

Mineral and vitamin intake is important for a dog's overall health and wellness. Just like humans, dogs need a balanced and nutritious diet to function optimally. If you are considering stopping store-bought dog food and providing natural sources of vitamins and minerals, it's important to understand the best mineral and vitamin intake for your dog and the natural sources that can provide these essential nutrients.

At the end of the book, in Chapter 14, I detail the average minimum and maximum amounts of vitamins and minerals. It really is very difficult to provide a hard-and-fast rule because dogs weights vary so much and different breeds will have differing strengths and weaknesses. Getting the correct amount for your own dog really is a question for your veterinary. However, I can provide information on why they matter and the recipes contain a variety of them as part of the ingredient lists.

PROTEINS, CARBS AND VITAMINS

Vitamins and Minerals

Dogs, like humans, require a balanced diet of vitamins and minerals for optimal health. These essential nutrients include vitamins A, D, E, K, B-complex vitamins, and minerals such as calcium, phosphorus, potassium, magnesium, iron, sodium, chlorine, copper, iodine, selenium, and zinc.

Vitamin A is important for good vision and a healthy immune system. Good natural sources of vitamin A include liver, sweet potatoes, carrots, and spinach.

Vitamin C is an antioxidant that protects your pup's body from free radicals and supports immune health. This vitamin can of course be found in oranges but also in organ meat.

Vitamin D helps the body absorb calcium and phosphorus, is essential for healthy bones and teeth. Dogs can synthesise vitamin D from exposure to sunlight, as well as fatty fish like salmon, tuna and sardines.

Vitamin E is an antioxidant that helps protect cells from damage supporting the immune system and essential for muscle and nerve function. Good natural sources of vitamin E include leafy greens, nuts, seeds and plant oils.

Vitamin K is also necessary for strong bones and blood clotting. Natural sources of vitamin K include spinach, kale, and broccoli. Most leafy green vegetables are a great source of Vitamin K.

Vitamin B represents 8 vitamins sometimes called **B-complex** vitamins. They help with energy production and the metabolism of carbohydrates, proteins, and fats. They support a healthy nervous system, and keeps your dogs coat looking fab. Good natural sources of B-complex vitamins include meat, poultry, fish, dairy products, rice and leafy greens.

Vitamin B12, for example, is important for nerve function and the production of red blood cells. Natural sources of Vitamin B12 include liver, kidney, and eggs.

Omega-3 Fatty Acids: These fatty acids are important for heart health, joint health, and skin and coat health. Good sources of Omega-3 fatty acids include salmon, flaxseed, and chia seeds.

Calcium is important for strong bones, teeth, nerve and muscle function, and proper blood clotting. Natural sources of calcium include dairy products such as yogurt and cottage cheese, as well as bone broth, sardines and leafy greens.

Copper this essential trace mineral supports healthy bones, connective tissue, and melanin production. it helps with the production of red blood cells and the metabolism of iron. It can be found in organ meats like liver, whole grains, legumes and leafy greens amongst others.

Phosphorus, this mineral works with calcium to maintain strong bones and it's also needed for energy production. Sources of phosphorus include meat, poultry, fish, dairy products, and whole grains.

Potassium and **Sodium** regulate fluid balance and aids in muscle and nerve function and helps maintains blood pressure. Good natural sources of potassium include bananas, sweet potatoes, and squash and sources of sodium include salt and table scraps from human foods that contain salt.

Magnesium maintains healthy bones, muscles, and nerves; aids in energy production and enzyme function as well as the metabolism of carbohydrates, proteins, and fats. It can be found in leafy greens, nuts, and seeds.

Manganese Helps metabolise proteins and carbohydrates and is essential for bone and cartilage formation. Fruit berries like blueberries, whole grains, leafy greens, legumes and just some sources of manganese.

Iron is important for the production of healthy red blood cells, which carry oxygen throughout the body. Good sources include red meat, poultry, and fish.

Chlorine helps regulate fluid balance and aids in digestion. Like Sodium, it is found in human foods that contain salt.

Iodine regulates the metabolism and is needed for the production of thyroid hormones. It can be found in iodized salt and seaweed.

Selenium protects cells from damage and is necessary for the proper functioning of the immune system. It works with vitamin E as an antioxidant, protecting your dog's cells from damage. Sources include Brazil nuts and liver.

Zinc is good for wound healing and the metabolism of carbohydrates, proteins, and fats and is involved in immunity, digestion, reproduction, and skin health. It can be found in meat, poultry, fish, dairy products, and whole grains.

Proteins and Carbs

In addition to these essential minerals and vitamins, dogs also need a balanced diet that includes protein, carbohydrates, and healthy fats.

First up, proteins. Dogs are carnivores at heart, which means their bodies thrive on protein. Think of it as the building block for their muscles, organs, and overall well-being. High-quality animal-based proteins like chicken, beef, turkey, and fish provide essential amino acids to keep your dog in tip-top shape.

Next, we've got fats. Good fats are essential for our pooches. They provide energy, promote healthy skin and coat, and help with vitamin absorption. Healthy fats include omega-3 and omega-6 fatty acids, which can be found in fish oil, flaxseed oil, and some plant oils.

Carbohydrates are another part of the canine nutrition equation. While dogs don't need carbs in the same way we do, they can still benefit from the energy and nutrients they provide. Plus, carbs can be great for dogs with food sensitivities or allergies. Think sweet potatoes, peas, or brown rice.

Examples of weight and food type

Let's dive deeper into the essential nutrients in our homemade recipes. In the following chapter I will provide examples of calories and the mix of proteins, carbs and fats before showing you a 7 meal plan that can last a month. I will show the ingredients and their specific benefits for dogs and we'll discuss the daily requirements for these nutrients and how a combination of recipes can help meet your dog's needs.

CHAPTER 5
7 DAY MENU FOR A MONTH OF DAILY MEALS

As a general guideline commercial dog foods typically contain carbohydrates which range from around 30% to 60% of the total caloric content in dog food, although it can go higher in certain brands (this is too high). Fats can range from around 10% to 25% of the total caloric content and proteins can range from around 20% to 40% of the total caloric content in manufactured dog food. Many mainstream commercial dog food manufacturers replace protein with carbohydrates to bring up the calorie count. This is why making your own dog food can be much better for your dog's health because you can control the levels of the 'right' caloric source and provide a better balance of fat, carbohydrate and protein.

The total caloric range for 33lb (15kg) average dog is between 750-950 calories a day. Generally the range is 23-30 calories per lb (50-65 calories per kilo). We will use grams of protein per portion and calories delivered by each source to create a balanced daily meal plan.

22   HEALTHY HOMEMADE DOG FOOD COOKBOOK & GUIDE

To provide a balanced diet in terms of nutrients and calories, dogs need the caloric mix to be around 30-40% protein, 40-45% carbohydrate and 15-20% fat.

Protein

Dogs need about 1 gram of protein per pound of body weight daily. For example, a 45-pound dog would need about 45 grams of protein per day. If you work in kilo's then there are 2.2lbs per kilo. Your dog would need 0.45 grams of protein per kilo. Whatever the case, you want to ensure that he gets a minimum of 10% protein in his daily diet. This isn't an exact science because all dogs are different but it is a useful to have some minimums!

Chicken is an excellent source of lean protein and essential amino acids. A 3.5-ounce (100-gram) serving of cooked chicken breast provides around 25-30 grams of protein and around 100-120 calories . Your 45lb dog would reach his 45 gram protein intake with around 180 grams of chicken, representing 160-180 calories with around 18% of his total calorie daily intake coming from protein. This would be within an acceptable range. 0f 15-30%. You don't want to be below 10% for protein in terms of its proportion of daily caloric intake.

Generally, lean ground beef (90% lean, 10% fat) contains around 20-25 grams of protein per 100 grams (3.5 oz). At 4 calories per gram of protein this would equate to 80-100 calories per 100 grams.

Salmon is not only a great protein source but also rich in omega-3 fatty acids, supporting skin, coat, and immune system health. A 3.5-ounce (100-gram) serving of cooked salmon contains around 25-30 grams of protein.

As you can see, as general rule of thumb you can work to 25-30 grams of protein per 100 grams of meat and 100 to 125 calories per 100 grams. For fish you can work to around 25 grams of protein per 100 grams (and 100 calories) although fish contains other nutrients and healthy fats which increase the calorie ratio.

While the caloric count of protein (at 4 calories per gram of protein) is a handy measure, it doesn't give us the entire picture. For example chicken (without the skin) has less fat than ground beef, so its overall calorie count is lower. It means that these are a useful guide to get an idea of calories and overall nutrients, and this can help when you are making your dog food and creating a daily or weekly menu plan - and it is still better than dealing with the unknown quantities in manufactured dog food.

I provide information on the protein an calorie content of the main foods used in the book at the end

Fats

The daily fat requirement for an average adult dog is about 10-15% of their daily caloric intake.

Flaxseed oil is an example of a 'good fat; because its a good source of omega-3 fatty acids, which promote healthy skin and coat, reduce inflammation, and support brain function.

Olive oil, another 'good fat' is high in monounsaturated fats and antioxidants, promoting heart health and immune system function.

Carbohydrates

Carbs should make up about 40-60% of an adult dog's daily caloric intake, but this may vary based on your dog's specific needs. Ideally, aiming for around 50% by weight. Your dogs carb content will also include around 3-5% fibre.

Brown rice is a complex carbohydrate, providing energy and fibre for healthy digestion. One cooked cup (195 grams) of brown rice contains around 220 calories. Based on a total daily calorie intake of say 900 calories, this would be 25% - about half of the daily requirement of between 40-60% carbs.

Sweet potatoes meanwhile are a nutrient-dense carb source packed with vitamins, minerals, and antioxidants. One medium-sized (115 grams) baked sweet potato provides about 100-110 calories and you can see that by combing both rice and sweet potato's as well as green veg you can easily get to the required amounts of carbs.

Fibre

Ideally you also want your dogs fibre intake to be between 5-7% or you dogs calorie intake and these are often contained in the calories on the food in which they are embedded, like rice for example.

Vitamins and minerals

The daily requirements for vitamins and minerals vary depending on the specific nutrient as well as the size of your dog. To ensure that your dog gets all the essential nutrients and vitamins, you can create a meal plan by combining different recipes for breakfast and dinner so that each day your dog is getting the right balance of nutrients over its daily meals.

For example, you might serve Chicken, brown rice, and vegetables for breakfast and salmon, quinoa, and mixed vegetables for dinner. This combination provides a variety of proteins, carbs, fats, and micronutrients to cover your dog's nutritional needs.

The number of meals your dog needs will also depend on the size, age, and activity level of your dog and, below, is a general guideline for daily feeding amounts based on your dog's weight - it is far from definitive so use it as a guide only. (Puppy's, for example, need a different diet to adult dogs and dog breed also play an important part.). In general it is based on roughly a 200 gram cup containing 350 calories.

The following will give you an idea of what to expect depending on your breed of dog.

- 20lbs: Beagle 20-30 pounds, Cocker Spaniel 25-35 pounds, French Bulldog 16-28 pounds, Staffordshire Bull Terrier 24-38 pounds, Welsh Corgi (Cardigan or Pembroke) 25-38 pounds,
- 45lbs: English Bulldog: 40-50 pounds, Basset Hound: 40-65 pounds, Standard Poodle: 45-70 pounds.
- 65 lbs: Labrador Retriever 55-80 pounds, Golden Retriever 55-75 pounds), German Shepherd 50-90 pounds, Boxer 50-80 pounds, Siberian Husky 35-60 pounds, Border Collie 30-55 pounds
- Smaller dogs include the Toy Poodle, 4-6 pounds and the Miniature Poodle, 10-15 pounds.
- Larger dogs include the Rottweiler at 80-100 pounds, Bernese Mountain Dog, 80-115 pounds, Doberman Pinscher,

26   HEALTHY HOMEMADE DOG FOOD COOKBOOK & GUIDE

75-100 pounds, Great Dane, 100-200 pounds (can vary significantly), and the Newfoundland:,100-150 pounds.

Finally, the last part of the jigsaw. How many grams should you feed your dog?

The common guideline is to feed approximately 2-3% of your dog's body weight in food per day.

Let's apply this to a 30-pound dog:

Minimum food amount = 2% of 30 pounds = 0.02 * 30 = 0.6 pounds (275 grams)

Maximum food amount = 3% of 30 pounds = 0.03 * 30 = o.09 pounds (410 grams)

So, a 30-pound dog would need to consume between 275 grams and 410 grams of dog food per day (between 0.6 and 0.9 pounds).

The following table gives you an idea of how this looks. I have taken the mid-point of the daily calorie requirement then applied the proportions of proteins, carbohydrate and fat. You want to try and get these percentages to a hundred across the day and over all his meals. Use it as a guide only. In some cases the protein percent might need to be higher but as a general rule don't go above 50%.

Weight	Daily Calories Reqts	Average Calorie as example	Daily Protein Calories @ 20-30%	Daily Carbs Calories @30-60%	Daily Fat Calories @10-20%	Cups of food/day (approx 200g/350 Calories per cup)	Weight food (min and max) per day
30 lbs (14 kg)	600-900	750	150-225	225-450	75-150	1.5 - 2	275-410 gms 0.9-1.35 lbs
45 lbs (20kg)	900-1400	1150	230-345	345-690	115-230	2 - 3	410-615 gms 0.9-1.3 lbs
65 lbs (30 kg)	1400-2000	1700	340-510	510-1020	170-340	3 - 4.5	590-890 gms 1.3-2lbs

7 MEALS FOR A MONTH

If this is the first time that you have changed your dogs food or tried homemade, then introduce the new food slowly over at least a few days. Changing you dogs food suddenly can sometimes upset their system. Try mixing in some of his current food with some of your homemade recipes to get his body acclimatised to his new menu. This won't take long, anywhere between 3 and 7 days.

The following recipes make more than one meal (unless you have an extra large dog). Rather than varying every day you could prepare a meal and use it until its finished. Each meal should last for 3-4 days (a little longer than you want to store in the refrigerator so pop some in the freezer if it stretches beyond 3 days).

If you have the total weight of the recipe, you can use a conversion factor to estimate the number of cups. For example, if you know that the recipe weighs 1200 grams and a cup of the prepared dog food weighs 200 grams, then the recipe would make approximately 6 cups of dog food (1200 grams ÷ 200 grams/cup = 6 cups).

To prepare the recipes and make more (or fewer) meals, you can easily scale up or down by changing all the ingredient amounts, then portioning and storing the prepared food in the refrigerator or freezer. It's always a good idea to let your veterinarian know that you are changing diet and to make sure there is nothing that they might be concerned about.

Don't forget to mix well and wait until the food is cool before giving it to your pooch

Day 1:

Breakfast: Beefy Green Delight

Dinner: Butchers Bonanza

Day 2:

Breakfast: Chicken & Veggie Power Bowl

Dinner: Salmon and Sweet Potato Mash

Day 3:

Breakfast: Turkey Superfood Scramble

Dinner: Lamb & Quinoa Goodness

Day 4:

Breakfast: Beefy Green Cottage Delight

Dinner: Butchers Bonanza

7 DAY MENU FOR A MONTH OF DAILY MEALS

Day 5:

Breakfast: Chicken & Veggie Power Bowl

Dinner: Salmon and Sweet Potato Mash

Day 6:

Breakfast: Turkey Superfood Scramble

Dinner: Lamb & Quinoa Goodness

Day 7:

Breakfast: Butchers Bonanza

Dinner: Turkey Superfood Scramble

In the first recipe I have added in the grams and calories. I don't do this for all the recipes but hopefully by including now and again it will help you get a feel for the weights and calories.

BEEFY GREEN COTTAGE DELIGHT

Yield: 6 cups of prepared food

Ingredients

- 1 lb lean ground beef (455 grams, 380-450 calories)
- 2 cups green beans, chopped (250 grams, 60-80 calories)
- 1 cup low-fat cottage cheese (125 grams, 150-175 calories)
- 1 cups cooked brown rice or quinoa (160 grams, 200-400 calories)
- 1 tablespoon ground flaxseed (40 calories)
- 1-2 teaspoon calcium supplement (powdered form, as recommended by your vet)

Instructions

1. Cook the ground beef in a skillet over medium heat until browned and cooked through. Drain any excess fat if needed.
2. Steam or boil the green beans until tender. Chop them into bite-sized pieces.
3. In a large mixing bowl, combine the cooked beef, green beans, cottage cheese, brown rice (or quinoa), ground flaxseed, and calcium supplement.
4. Mix everything thoroughly and serve when cool

CHICKEN & VEGGIE POWER BOWL

Yield: 6 cups of prepared food

Ingredients

- 1 lb boneless, skinless chicken breast or thighs, cooked and shredded
- 2 cups sweet potatoes, cubed and cooked
- 2 cups green beans, chopped and cooked
- 1 cup cooked brown rice or quinoa
- 1 tablespoon fish oil or olive oil
- 1 teaspoon calcium supplement (powdered form, as recommended by your vet)

Instructions

1. Steam or boil the sweet potatoes until tender. You can also bake them in the oven at 400°F (205°C) for about 40-45 minutes or until tender.
2. Steam or boil the green beans until tender.
3. Cook the chicken breast or thighs by boiling or baking until fully cooked, then shred the meat.
4. In a large mixing bowl, combine the shredded chicken, cooked sweet potatoes, cooked green beans, cooked brown rice (or quinoa), fish oil (or olive oil), and calcium supplement.
5. Mix everything thoroughly and let it cool before serving it to your dog.

BUTCHERS BONANZA

Yield: 8-10 cups of prepared food

Ingredients

- 2 lbs cooked beef (you can replace with chopped or ground chicken, or turkey)
- 2 cups cooked mixed vegetables (e.g. carrots, green beans, sweet potatoes), finely chopped or mashed
- 2 cups cooked brown rice or quinoa
- 1 tbsp fish oil or olive oil
- 1/4 tsp dried rosemary

Instructions

1. Cook the meat, vegetables, and rice or quinoa separately according to their respective instructions. Allow to cool, then finely chop or mash the vegetables and the meat.
2. Combine the cooked and chopped meat, vegetables, and rice or quinoa in a mixing bowl.
3. Add the fish oil or olive oil and dried rosemary to the bowl, then mix well to combine.
4. Divide the mixture into individual portions based on your dog's daily feeding needs.
5. Serve fresh or store any leftovers in an airtight container

Adding turmeric to your dog's homemade meal can also offer some extra health benefits. Turmeric contains a compound called curcumin, which has anti-inflammatory, antioxidant, and potential anti-cancer properties. These benefits can help support your dog's joint health, boost their immune system, and improve their overall wellbeing.

To include turmeric in the recipe I provided above you can follow these guidelines:

1. Start with a small amount: For a dog of average size, begin with 1/8 to 1/4 teaspoon of turmeric powder per day, mixed into their food. You can gradually increase the amount to around 1/2 teaspoon per day, based on your dog's size and tolerance.
2. Combine with black pepper: Adding a pinch of black pepper can enhance the absorption of curcumin in your dog's body. Black pepper contains a compound called piperine, which can increase the bioavailability of curcumin by up to 2000%.
3. Mix with a healthy fat: Curcumin is fat-soluble, so combining it with a healthy fat, such as the ground flaxseed already in the recipe, can improve absorption.
4. Serve fresh or store in your refrigerator or freezer.

SAVORY SALMON MEDLEY

Yield: 8-10 cups of prepared food

Ingredients

- 2 lbs salmon fillets, cooked and flaked
- 2 cups green beans, cooked and chopped
- 2 cups carrots, cooked and chopped
- 2 cups spinach, cooked and chopped
- 1/4 tsp turmeric powder
- 1 tbsp ground flaxseed
- 1 tsp fish oil or olive oil

Instructions

1. Cook the salmon fillets until fully cooked and flaky. Allow to cool and remove any bones or skin, then flake the salmon meat into small pieces.
2. Cook the green beans, carrots, and spinach until tender. Allow to cool, then chop into small pieces.
3. Mix the cooked and chopped vegetables with the cooked and flaked salmon.
4. Add the turmeric powder, ground flaxseed, and fish oil or olive oil to the bowl, then mix well to combine.
5. Divide the mixture into individual portions.

TURKEY SUPERFOOD SCRAMBLE

Yield: 4-6 cups of prepared food

Ingredients

- 1 lb ground turkey
- 1/2 cup cooked quinoa
- 1/2 cup cooked mixed vegetables (e.g. carrots, green beans, broccoli), finely chopped or mashed
- 1/2 cup blueberries
- 1 tbsp olive oil
- 1/4 tsp dried parsley

Instructions

1. In a large skillet, heat the olive oil over medium heat.
2. Add the ground turkey to the skillet and cook until browned, breaking it up into small pieces as it cooks.
3. Add the cooked quinoa, mixed vegetables, blueberries, and dried parsley to the skillet, and stir well to combine.
4. Cook for an additional 3-4 minutes, until the vegetables are slightly softened and the blueberries have burst.
5. Remove from heat and cool before serving in individual portions

LAMB & QUINOA GOODNESS

Yield: 4-6 cups of prepared food

Ingredients

- 1 pound ground lamb
- 1 cup cooked quinoa
- 1/2 cup chopped carrots
- 1/2 cup chopped green beans
- 1/4 cup chopped parsley
- 2 tablespoons olive oil

Instructions

1. Preheat the oven to 375°F (190°C).
2. In a large bowl, combine the ground lamb, cooked quinoa, chopped carrots, chopped green beans, chopped parsley, and olive oil. Mix well.
3. Roll the mixture into small balls, each about the size of a ping-pong ball.
4. Place the balls on a baking sheet lined with parchment paper.
5. Bake in the preheated oven for 20-25 minutes, or until the lamb is cooked through.
6. Let the lamb and quinoa mixture to cool before serving to your dog.

SALMON AND SWEET POTATO MASH

Yield: 8-10 cups of prepared food

Ingredients

- 1 pound salmon fillet, cooked and shredded
- 2 cups cooked sweet potato, mashed
- 1 cup green beans, steamed and chopped
- 1 tablespoon fish oil
- 1/2 teaspoon dried parsley
- 1/2 teaspoon dried dill
- 1/2 teaspoon dried oregano

Instructions

1. Preheat the oven to 350°F.
2. In a large bowl, mix the cooked and shredded salmon with the mashed sweet potato.
3. Add the chopped green beans, fish oil, and dried herbs to the bowl and mix well.
4. Spoon the mixture into a baking dish and bake for 25-30 minutes.
5. Cool before serving.

Based on the amounts of ingredients listed in the recipes, the total amount of prepared meals produced should be around 44-54 cups. If your dog uses around 1.5-2 cups per day (300-400 grams) then these meals would last for around 29-36 days.

You can mix and match almost all of the recipes in this book but if you have a healthy adult dog then don't only use the recipes in the puppy and senior dog chapters. They are either high in protein or lower in carbs to suit the ages of these dogs. You want to ensure that your pup is getting a balanced amount of both in his diet and that meets his needs. Be sure to try all the other recipes and add them into a broad menu that meets your own dogs needs and tastes!

CHAPTER 6

SINGLE MEAL ADULT DOG RECIPES

This is great if you have any leftovers from your own meals and you want to incorporate them into a healthy meal for your dog.

TURKEY AND QUINOA BOWL

- 1 cup ground turkey, cooked (about 200 to 220 grams: Lean protein source, high in vitamins and minerals
- 1 cup cooked quinoa: High in protein, gluten-free, and rich in essential amino acids
- 1 cup steamed peas: Good source of vitamins A, K, and B, as well as fiber and protein

Cook ground turkey in a non-stick pan until fully cooked. Prepare quinoa according to package instructions. Steam peas until tender. Add everything into a bowl and mix it together. Once done, its ready to eat.

BEEF AND CHICKPEA STEW

- 1 cup lean ground beef, cooked: Protein source, rich in iron and B vitamins
- 1 cup cooked chickpeas: High in fiber, protein, and essential nutrients like folate and manganese
- 1 cup diced carrots, steamed: High in vitamin A for eye health and a good source of fiber

Cook ground beef in a non-stick pan until fully cooked. Cook chickpeas according to package instructions. Steam carrots until tender then add and mix the ingredients together before serving.

LENTIL AND VEGGIE MIX

- 1 cup cooked lentils: High in protein, fiber, and essential nutrients like iron and folate
- 1 cup diced zucchini, steamed: Low in calories, high in fiber and antioxidants
- 1 cup diced bell peppers, steamed: High in vitamin C and antioxidants

Cook lentils according to package instructions. Steam zucchini and bell peppers until tender. Mix all the ingredients together and serve.

SINGLE MEAL ADULT DOG RECIPES

EGG AND SPINACH SCRAMBLE

- 2 large eggs, scrambled: High-quality protein source, rich in vitamins and minerals
- 1 cup steamed spinach: High in vitamins A, C, and K, as well as iron and antioxidants
- 1 cup cooked, mashed pumpkin: High in fiber and a good source of vitamins A and C

Scramble eggs in a non-stick pan. Steam spinach until wilted. Cook pumpkin until tender, then mash and mix it all together. Once done, it's ready to eat.

FISH AND GREEN PEA MEDLEY

- 1 cup whitefish or sardines, cooked and flaked: Rich in omega-3 fatty acids, high-quality protein source
- 1 cup cooked, mashed sweet potatoes: High in fiber, beta-carotene, and vitamins B6 and C
- 1 cup steamed peas: Good source of vitamins A, K, and B, as well as fiber and protein

Cook fish until fully cooked, then flake. Cook sweet potatoes until tender, then mash. Steam peas until tender. Mix together then pop it in your dogs' bowl.

TURKEY AND PUMPKIN STEW

- 1 cup ground turkey, cooked: Lean protein source, high in vitamins and minerals
- 1 cup cooked, mashed pumpkin: High in fiber and a good source of vitamins A and C
- 1 cup steamed zucchini, cubed: Low in calories, high in fiber and antioxidants

Cook ground turkey in a non-stick pan until fully cooked. Cook pumpkin until tender, then mash. Steam zucchini until tender, then cube. Mix all the ingredients together and its ready to eat.

DUCK AND GREEN BEAN BOWL

- 1 cup ground duck, cooked: High in protein, essential vitamins and minerals, and a novel protein source for allergy-prone dogs
- 1 cup steamed green beans: Low in calories, source of vitamins A, C, and K
- 1 cup cooked, mashed butternut squash: High in fiber, vitamins A and C, and potassium

Cook ground duck in a non-stick pan until fully cooked. Steam green beans until tender. Cook butternut squash until tender, then mash. Mix everything together.

TURKEY AND QUINOA BOWL

- 1 cup ground turkey, cooked: Lean protein source, high in vitamins and minerals
- 1 cup cooked quinoa: High in protein, gluten-free, and rich in essential amino acids
- 1 cup steamed peas: Good source of vitamins A, K, and B, as well as fiber and protein

Cook ground turkey in a non-stick pan until fully cooked. Prepare quinoa according to package instructions. Steam peas until tender. Mix and serve.

These recipes provide a single serving and can be scaled up or down depending on your dog's size and caloric needs.

CHAPTER 7
RECIPES FOR COMMON CONDITIONS

n this chapter we cover some of the most common problems that you may have with your dog over the course of his or her life.

Although I highlight each recipe in terms of a particular condition, these recipes can be used for any healthy adult dog by adding them into a mix of daily or weekly meals.

In these recipes I include the vitamins in each ingredient.

PROTEIN ALLERGIES

Some dogs may develop allergies or sensitivities to specific protein sources, such as chicken or beef. A homemade diet allows for more control over protein selection, enabling you to choose alternative sources like fish, venison, or turkey that your dog may tolerate better.

RECIPES FOR COMMON CONDITIONS   45

FOOD SENSITIVITIES

Dogs can develop sensitivities to certain ingredients, resulting in digestive issues or skin problems. Some dogs may develop intolerances or sensitivities to specific ingredients, such as dairy, eggs, or certain proteins, and of course grain or wheat. A homemade diet means that you can avoid potential triggers and cater to individual sensitivities, and you can choose from many of the recipes in the book to find ones that avoid any intolerances.

Sensitivities to eggs or dairy is fairly easy to manage (and is often the result of lactose intolerance) but grain free tends to me more common. I will cover grain-free here (which also includes wheat).

Grain or wheat free

As you might expect symptoms of a grain sensitivity or allergy display in one or more ways. I have highlighted some common symptoms that you might see in your dog if he has a wheat or grain allergy/sensitivity. In my case, my dog displayed skin irritation (and displayed dandruff), an ear infection and was constantly licking or chewing of her paws.

- Skin irritation or inflammation (redness, hot spots, itching)
- Hair loss or excessive shedding
- Ear infections or chronic ear inflammation
- Gastrointestinal issues (diarrhea, vomiting, gas, or changes in stool consistency)
- Frequent licking or chewing of paws and skin
- Skin sores or scabs
- Respiratory issues (sneezing, coughing, or wheezing)

46   HEALTHY HOMEMADE DOG FOOD COOKBOOK & GUIDE

It may be difficult to determine whether your dog needs a wheat-free or grain-free diet based on the symptoms alone, as the symptoms can be quite similar. A visit to your veterinarian is recommended and your vet may suggest an elimination diet, blood tests, or skin tests to help identify the specific allergen causing the issue.

Why Grain-Free Packaged Dog Food Can Be Harmful

Over the past decade, there's been a rise in popularity for packaged dry or wet grain-free dog food, marketed as a healthier option for dogs.

The idea behind grain-free food is that dogs evolved to eat a diet of mostly meat, and that grains are an unnatural and unhealthy addition to their diet.

However, grain-free diets are not always the best choice for every dog. Some grain-free diets are made with more fat, protein, and calories, which can be harmful to dogs who are overweight or have health issues such as pancreatitis.

Studies have also shown that grain-free dog food can lead to a condition called dilated cardiomyopathy (DCM), a type of heart disease that can cause heart failure and in 2018, the U.S. Food and Drug Administration (FDA) began investigating reports of DCM in dogs that were fed a grain-free diet. The investigation revealed that dogs fed a diet that was high in legumes such as peas, lentils, and potatoes were more likely to develop DCM.

Grains are a rich source of important nutrients such as fiber, vitamins, and minerals. For example, rice and barley are good sources of vitamins, including B vitamins, iron, and zinc and

RECIPES FOR COMMON CONDITIONS

without these ingredients, grain-free diets may lack the balance of nutrients that dogs need.

The following recipes provide a better balance than many of the packaged grain-free foods that you can buy in a store.

These recipes are based on a single serving to give you an idea of how to prepare a single meal rather than batch cooking. They can be scaled up or down depending on your dog's size and caloric needs and, this time, I indicate each ingredient's benefits to help you understand their specific nutritional benefits.

CHICKEN AND SWEET POTATO MASH

- 1 cup boiled chicken, shredded
- Rich in protein for muscle maintenance and growth
- 1 cup cooked sweet potatoes, mashed: High in fiber, beta-carotene, and vitamins B6 and C
- 1 cup steamed green beans: Low in calories, source of vitamins A, C, and K

Boil chicken until fully cooked, then shred. Cook sweet potatoes until tender, then mash. Steam green beans until tender. Mix all ingredients together.

GRAIN-FREE SALMON AND VEGETABLE MEDLEY

- 1 cup baked or steamed salmon, flaked: High in omega-3 fatty acids for healthy skin and coat
- 1 cup steamed broccoli: Source of vitamins K, C, and A, as well as fiber and potassium
- 1 cup cooked, mashed cauliflower: Low in calories, high in fiber, and a good source of vitamins C and K

Bake or steam salmon until fully cooked, then flake. Steam broccoli and cauliflower until tender. Mash the cauliflower. Mix all ingredients together.

BEEF AND CHICKPEA STEW

- 1 cup lean ground beef, cooked: Protein source, rich in iron and B vitamins
- 1 cup cooked chickpeas: High in fiber, protein, and essential nutrients like folate and manganese
- 1 cup diced carrots, steamed: High in vitamin A for eye health and a good source of fiber

Cook ground beef in a non-stick pan until fully cooked. Cook chickpeas according to package instructions. Steam carrots until tender. Mix all ingredients together.

LENTIL AND VEGGIE MIX

- 1 cup cooked lentils: High in protein, fiber, and essential nutrients like iron and folate
- 1 cup diced zucchini, steamed: Low in calories, high in fiber and antioxidants
- 1 cup diced bell peppers, steamed: High in vitamin C and antioxidants

Cook lentils according to package instructions. Steam zucchini and bell peppers until tender. Mix all ingredients together.

EGG AND SPINACH SCRAMBLE

- 2 large eggs, scrambled: High-quality protein source, rich in vitamins and minerals
- 1 cup steamed spinach: High in vitamins A, C, and K, as well as iron and antioxidants
- 1 cup cooked, mashed pumpkin: High in fiber and a good source of vitamins A and C

Scramble eggs in a non-stick pan. Steam spinach until wilted. Cook pumpkin until tender, then mash. Mix all ingredients together.

FISH AND GREEN PEA MEDLEY

- 1 cup whitefish or sardines, cooked and flaked: Rich in omega-3 fatty acids, high-quality protein source
- 1 cup cooked, mashed sweet potatoes: High in fiber, beta-carotene, and vitamins B6 and C
- 1 cup steamed peas: Good source of vitamins A, K, and B, as well as fiber and protein

Cook fish until fully cooked, then flake. Cook sweet potatoes until tender, then mash. Steam peas until tender. Mix all ingredients together.

TURKEY AND PUMPKIN STEW

- 1 cup ground turkey, cooked: Lean protein source, high in vitamins and minerals
- 1 cup cooked, mashed pumpkin: High in fiber and a good source of vitamins A and C
- 1 cup steamed zucchini, cubed: Low in calories, high in fiber and antioxidants

Cook ground turkey in a non-stick pan until fully cooked. Cook pumpkin until tender, then mash. Steam zucchini until tender, then cube. Mix all ingredients together.

DUCK AND GREEN BEAN BOWL

- 1 cup ground duck, cooked: High in protein, essential vitamins and minerals, and a novel protein source for allergy-prone dogs
- 1 cup steamed green beans: Low in calories, source of vitamins A, C, and K
- 1 cup cooked, mashed butternut squash: High in fiber, vitamins A and C, and potassium

Cook ground duck in a non-stick pan until fully cooked. Steam green beans until tender. Cook butternut squash until tender, then mash. Mix all ingredients together.

WEIGHT MANAGEMENT

Obesity is a common problem in dogs, which can lead to various health issues. It can lead to increased risks of joint problems, heart disease, and other health complications. A homemade diet means that you can get precise control over portion sizes and the selection of lean proteins, healthy fats, and low-glycemic carbohydrates to support weight management.

Turkey and rabbit are great sources of protein if you have a dog that needs a little bit of weight management.

LEAN TURKEY AND VEGETABLE STEW

Yield: 4 Cups

Ingredients

- 1 lb lean ground turkey (protein)
- 2 cups mixed vegetables (carrots, green beans, zucchini) (fiber, vitamins A, C)
- 1 cup sweet potatoes, diced (fiber, vitamins A, B6)
- 1 tablespoon coconut oil (healthy fat)

Instructions

1. In a large pot, heat the coconut oil over medium heat.
2. Add the ground turkey and cook until browned and cooked through.
3. Add the mixed vegetables and sweet potatoes to the pot and stir well.
4. Cover the pot and simmer for about 15 minutes or until the vegetables are tender. Cool and serve.

RECIPES FOR COMMON CONDITIONS 53

This stew is low in fat, making it suitable for dogs who need to lose weight. The lean ground turkey provides a good source of protein, while the mixed vegetables and sweet potatoes offer fiber and essential vitamins.

SALMON AND QUINOA SALAD

Yield: 3 Cups

Ingredients

- 1 lb boneless salmon fillets (protein, omega-3 fatty acids)
- 1 cup cooked quinoa (protein, fiber)
- 1 cup cucumber, diced (hydration, vitamins K, C)
- 1/2 cup cherry tomatoes, halved (antioxidants, vitamins A, C)
- 1 tablespoon lemon juice (vitamin C)

Instructions

1. Preheat the oven to 400°F (200°C). Place the salmon fillets on a baking sheet lined with parchment paper and bake for 12-15 minutes or until cooked through.
2. Remove the salmon from the oven and let it cool. Flake the salmon into small pieces.
3. In a mixing bowl, combine the cooked quinoa, diced cucumber, cherry tomatoes, and flaked salmon.
4. Drizzle the lemon juice over the salad and toss gently to combine.
5. Serve the salmon and quinoa salad chilled.

This is a nutritious and low-calorie option for overweight dogs. The salmon provides high-quality protein and essential omega-3 fatty acids, while the quinoa offers additional protein and fiber.

RECIPES FOR COMMON CONDITIONS   55

CHICKEN AND GREEN BEAN STIR-FRY

Yield: 4 Cups

Ingredients

- 1lb boneless, skinless chicken breasts, thinly sliced (protein)
- 2 cups green beans, trimmed and halved (fiber, vitamins A, C, K)
- 1 cup bell peppers, sliced (vitamin C)
- 1/2 cup low-sodium chicken broth (hydration)
- 1 tablespoon olive oil (healthy fat)
- 1 teaspoon low-sodium soy sauce (optional)

Instructions

1. Heat the olive oil in a large skillet or wok over medium-high heat.
2. Add the sliced chicken breasts to the skillet and cook until browned and cooked through.
3. Remove the chicken from the skillet and set aside.
4. In the same skillet, add the green beans and bell peppers. Stir-fry for a few minutes until the vegetables are crisp-tender.
5. Add the chicken broth to the skillet and simmer for a few more minutes to allow the flavors to blend.
6. Return the cooked chicken to the skillet and toss to combine with the vegetables and broth.
7. If desired, add the low-sodium soy sauce for additional flavor.

56   HEALTHY HOMEMADE DOG FOOD COOKBOOK & GUIDE

8. Remove from heat and let the stir-fry cool before serving to your dog.

This chicken and green bean stir-fry is a low-fat and low-calorie option that provides lean protein from chicken and fiber from green beans. The dish is packed with vitamins A, C, and K from the vegetables. The minimal use of oil and low-sodium soy sauce keeps the fat and sodium content low, making it suitable for dogs watching their weight.

RECIPES FOR COMMON CONDITIONS   57

TURKEY MEATBALL SOUP

Yield: 6 Cups

Ingredients

- 1 lb ground turkey (protein)
- 1 cup carrots, diced (fiber, beta-carotene)
- 1 cup celery, diced (fiber, vitamin K)
- 1 cup green peas (fiber, vitamin C)
- 4 cups low-sodium chicken broth (hydration)
- 1 tablespoon olive oil (healthy fat)
- 1 teaspoon dried parsley (antioxidants)

Instructions

1. In a large pot, heat the olive oil over medium heat.
2. Form the ground turkey into small meatballs and add them to the pot. Cook until browned on all sides.
3. Add the diced carrots, celery, and green peas to the pot and stir well.
4. Pour in the chicken broth and bring to a boil. Reduce the heat and simmer for about 20 minutes or until the vegetables are tender.
5. Sprinkle the dried parsley over the soup and stir and let it cool.

This soup is lower in fat and calories compared to traditional meatball soups. Soups are also great if your pup has been off his food and you are slowly re-introducing meals.

VEGETABLE AND LENTIL STEW

Yield: 5 Cups

Ingredients

- 1 cup lentils, rinsed and drained (protein, fiber)
- 2 cups mixed vegetables (carrots, peas, sweet potatoes) (fiber, vitamins A, C)
- 1 cup butternut squash, diced (fiber, vitamins A, C)
- 4 cups low-sodium vegetable broth (hydration)
- 1 tablespoon coconut oil (healthy fat)
- 1 teaspoon dried thyme (antioxidants)

Instructions

1. In a large pot, heat the coconut oil over medium heat.
2. Add the lentils, mixed vegetables, and butternut squash to the pot. Stir well to coat the vegetables
3. Pour in the low-sodium vegetable broth and bring to a boil. Reduce the heat and simmer for about 30-40 minutes, or until the lentils and vegetables are tender.
4. Sprinkle the dried thyme over the stew and stir to incorporate the flavors. Allow time to cool.

The lentils provide a good source of plant-based protein and fiber, while the mixed vegetables and butternut squash offer a variety of vitamins and minerals. The low-sodium vegetable broth keeps the sodium content low. It's a filling and satisfying meal that can help your dog feel satisfied while managing their weight.

DIGESTIVE DISORDERS

Dogs with sensitive stomachs, gastrointestinal disorders, or conditions like pancreatitis may benefit from a homemade diet that is carefully crafted to be easily digestible and gentle on their digestive system. It can help eliminate potential triggers like artificial additives, fillers, or preservatives, which can all contribute to digestive upset.

Here are a few recipes for sensitive tummy's.

SENSITIVE STOMACH PORK AND VEGETABLE STIR-FRY

Yield: 6 Cups

Ingredients

- 2 lbs lean pork, thinly sliced (protein, vitamins B6, B12, iron, zinc)
- 2 cups mixed vegetables (carrots, bell peppers, snap peas, broccoli), sliced (fiber, vitamins A, C, K)
- 1 cup brown rice, cooked (fiber, vitamins B1, B3, iron)
- 2 tablespoons low-sodium soy sauce (sodium)
- 1 tablespoon olive oil (fat)

Instructions

1. In a large skillet or wok, heat olive oil over medium-high heat.
2. Add the sliced pork and stir-fry until browned and cooked through.
3. Remove the pork from the skillet and set aside.
4. In the same skillet, add the mixed vegetables and stir-fry until crisp-tender.
5. Return the cooked pork to the skillet and add the cooked brown rice.
6. Drizzle the low-sodium soy sauce over the mixture and toss well to combine.
7. Continue stir-frying for a couple of minutes until everything is heated through.
8. Remove from heat and let it cool before serving to your dog.

RECIPES FOR COMMON CONDITIONS

Why it's Good for Dogs with Sensitive Stomachs or Gastrointestinal Disorders

This homemade stir-fry recipe is carefully crafted to provide a balance of easily digestible protein, fiber-rich vegetables, and gentle carbohydrates. It is free from common allergens, such as grains and dairy, which can trigger sensitivities in some dogs.

The lean pork is a lean protein source that is less likely to cause stomach upset compared to fattier meats. The mixed vegetables and brown rice offer a blend of fiber and nutrients that support digestive health and promote regular bowel movements. The low-sodium soy sauce adds flavor without excessive sodium, which can be beneficial for dogs with gastrointestinal sensitivities. The use of olive oil in moderation provides a healthy fat source that aids in nutrient absorption and supports a healthy coat.

TURKEY AND RICE DELIGHT

Yield: 4 Cups

Ingredients

- 2 cups cooked turkey, shredded (protein, vitamins B6, B12, iron, zinc)
- 1 cup cooked white rice (carbohydrates, fiber)
- 1/2 cup cooked carrots, diced (fiber, vitamins A, K)
- 1/2 cup cooked green beans, chopped (fiber, vitamins C, K)
- 1 tablespoon olive oil (healthy fat)

Instructions

1. In a bowl, combine the shredded turkey, cooked rice, carrots, and green beans.
2. Drizzle the olive oil over the mixture and mix well to coat all ingredients evenly.
3. Serve the desired portion size to your dog, adjusting based on their size and dietary need

SALMON AND SWEET POTATO MEDLEY

Yield: 3 -4 Cups

Ingredients

- 2 cups cooked salmon, flaked (protein, omega-3 fatty acids)
- 1 cup cooked sweet potato, mashed (carbohydrates, fiber, vitamins A, C)
- 1/2 cup cooked peas (fiber, vitamins K, C)
- 1/4 cup cooked quinoa (protein, fiber)
- 1 tablespoon coconut oil (healthy fat)

Instructions

1. In a mixing bowl, combine the flaked salmon, mashed sweet potato, cooked peas, and quinoa.
2. Add the coconut oil and mix well to incorporate all ingredients thoroughly.
3. Serve the appropriate portion size to your dog, considering their size and nutritional needs.

64   HEALTHY HOMEMADE DOG FOOD COOKBOOK & GUIDE

BEEF AND VEGETABLE STEW

Yield: 5-6 Cups

Ingredients

- 1 lb lean beef, diced (protein, vitamins B6, B12, iron)
- 2 cups low-sodium beef broth (hydration, flavor)
- 1 cup butternut squash, cubed (fiber, vitamins A, C)
- 1/2 cup peas (fiber, vitamins K, C)
- 1/2 cup carrots, sliced (fiber, vitamins A, K)

Instructions

1. In a large pot, brown the diced beef over medium heat.
2. Add the beef broth, butternut squash, peas, and carrots to the pot.
3. Simmer for about 20-25 minutes until the vegetables are tender and the beef is cooked through.
4. Remove from heat and drizzle the flaxseed oil over the stew, stirring well to combine.

RECIPES FOR COMMON CONDITIONS

FISH AND SWEET POTATO MASH

Yield: 3-4 Cups

Ingredients

- 2 cups cooked white fish (such as cod or haddock), flaked (protein, omega-3 fatty acids)
- 1 cup cooked sweet potato, mashed (carbohydrates, fiber, vitamins A, C)
- 1/2 cup cooked green peas (fiber, vitamins K, C)
- 1/4 cup cooked brown rice (fiber, B vitamins)
- 1 tablespoon coconut oil (healthy fat)

Instructions

1. In a bowl, combine the flaked white fish, mashed sweet potato, green peas, and cooked brown rice.
2. Add the coconut oil and mix well to incorporate all ingredients thoroughly.

These recipes are formulated to be gentle on the stomach and suitable for dogs with sensitive stomachs or gastrointestinal disorders. The ingredients chosen are generally easy to digest and provide beneficial nutrients to support overall health and well-being.

URINARY TRACT HEALTH

Certain homemade diets can help promote urinary tract health, especially in dogs prone to urinary issues or bladder stones. Ingredients like cranberries or blueberries can provide natural antioxidants and help maintain a healthy urinary pH.

The recipes on the next few pages are designed with urinary tract health in mind. Each recipe includes a balance of protein, low-purine carbohydrates, and healthy fats, along with beneficial ingredients such as cranberries, parsley, and fish oil that support urinary health.

The portion sizes mentioned in each recipe yield approximately 3-4 cups of prepared dog food but you can adjust the portion according to your dog's specific needs.

CHICKEN AND QUINOA DELIGHT

Yield: 3-4 Cups

Ingredients

- 2 cups cooked chicken breast, shredded (protein, B vitamins)
- 1 cup cooked quinoa (low-purine carbohydrate, fiber)
- 1/2 cup cooked carrots, finely chopped (vitamin A, antioxidants)
- 1/4 cup fresh parsley, chopped (natural diuretic, supports urinary health)
- 1 tablespoon olive oil (healthy fat)

Instructions

1. In a bowl, combine the shredded chicken breast, cooked quinoa, chopped carrots, and fresh parsley.
2. Drizzle the olive oil over the mixture and toss well to combine all ingredients.

68   HEALTHY HOMEMADE DOG FOOD COOKBOOK & GUIDE

SALMON AND SWEET POTATO STEW

Yield: 3-4 Cups

Ingredients:

- 2 cups cooked salmon, flaked (omega-3 fatty acids, protein)
- 1 cup cooked sweet potato, mashed (low-purine carbohydrate, vitamins A, C)
- 1/2 cup green beans, chopped (fiber, antioxidants)
- 1/4 cup cooked quinoa (low-purine carbohydrate, fiber)
- 1 tablespoon coconut oil (healthy fat)

Instructions

1. In a bowl, combine the flaked salmon, mashed sweet potato, chopped green beans, and cooked quinoa.
2. Add the coconut oil and mix well to incorporate all ingredients thoroughly.

RECIPES FOR COMMON CONDITIONS 69

TURKEY AND CRANBERRY DELIGHT

Yield: 3-4 Cups

Ingredients

- 2 cups cooked ground turkey, lean (protein, low-fat)
- 1 cup cooked brown rice (low-purine carbohydrate, fiber)
- 1/4 cup cranberries, fresh or dried (supports urinary tract health)
- 1/4 cup cooked green peas (fiber, antioxidants)
- 1 tablespoon flaxseed oil (omega-3 fatty acids)

Instructions

1. In a bowl, combine the cooked ground turkey, cooked brown rice, cranberries, and cooked green peas.
2. Drizzle the flaxseed oil over the mixture and mix well to incorporate all ingredients.

BEEF AND BARLEY STEW

Yield: 3-4 Cups

Ingredients

- 2 cups cooked lean beef, cubed (protein, vitamins B12, iron)
- 1 cup cooked barley (low-purine carbohydrate, fiber)
- 1/2 cup diced zucchini (hydrating, supports urinary health)
- 1/4 cup cooked carrots, diced (vitamin A, antioxidants)
- 1 tablespoon fish oil (omega-3 fatty acids)

Instructions

1. In a bowl, combine the cubed lean beef, cooked barley, diced zucchini, and diced carrots.
2. Drizzle the fish oil over the mixture and toss well to incorporate all ingredients.

RECIPES FOR COMMON CONDITIONS

TUNA AND CHICKPEA SALAD

Yield: 3-4 Cups

Ingredients

- 2 cups canned tuna in water, drained (protein, omega-3 fatty acids)
- 1 cup cooked chickpeas (low-purine carbohydrate, fiber)
- 1/2 cup cucumber
- 1/4 cup fresh cilantro, chopped (natural diuretic, supports urinary 1 tablespoon lemon juice (alkalizing, promotes urinary tract health)
- 1 tablespoon olive oil (healthy fat)

Instructions

1. In a bowl, combine the drained tuna, cooked chickpeas, chopped cucumber, and fresh cilantro.
2. Drizzle the lemon juice and olive oil over the mixture and toss well to combine.

SKIN AND COAT ISSUES

Dogs with skin allergies, dry skin, or dull coats can benefit from a homemade diet rich in omega-3 fatty acids, which are found in fish, flaxseed, or chia seeds. These nutrients can help improve skin health and promote a shiny coat.

If your dog has a skin allergy then identifying and eliminating potential allergens from the diet, such as certain proteins or grains, can help alleviate symptoms.

DENTAL HEALTH:

Homemade diets that include appropriate textures, such as raw meaty bones or dental chews made from natural ingredients, can help maintain dental health by reducing plaque buildup and promoting good oral hygiene.

Problems, such as tartar buildup or gum disease, are common in dogs. Healthy dog treats are a great way to combat this using tooth-friendly ingredients like crunchy vegetables which can help good oral hygiene. I will include a couple of examples in the Dog Treat chapter.

JOINT HEALTH:

Arthritis and joint conditions are very common, especially in senior dogs or larger breeds (although I have a cocker with hip problems, most likely early hip dysplasia and another older cocker with both arthritis and dysplasia).

Providing a diet rich in omega-3 fatty acids, glucosamine, and chondroitin through ingredients like fish, shellfish, and bone

RECIPES FOR COMMON CONDITIONS
73

broth can support joint health and alleviate discomfort. For me, shellfish is out, as I tend to avoid this with my cockers.

Here are some recipes you can try that are designed for dogs with poor bone health or conditions such as hip dysplasia. Each ingredient's benefits are outlined to help you understand their specific nutritional contribution to bone health and joint support.

CHICKEN AND OATMEAL WITH BLUEBERRIES

- 1 cup boiled chicken, shredded: High-quality protein for muscle maintenance
- 1 cup cooked oatmeal: Rich in fiber, vitamins, and minerals
- 1/2 cup blueberries: Antioxidants for immune support
- 1 tbsp ground flaxseed: Omega-3 fatty acids for joint health

Boil chicken until fully cooked, then shred. Cook oatmeal according to package instructions. Mix all ingredients together, adding flaxseed and blueberries.

SARDINE AND SWEET POTATO MASH

- 1 cup canned sardines (in water), drained: Rich in omega-3 fatty acids for joint health
- 1 cup cooked sweet potatoes, mashed: High in fiber, beta-carotene, and vitamins B6 and C
- 1 cup steamed green beans: Low in calories, source of vitamins A, C, and K

Drain canned sardines. Cook sweet potatoes until tender, then mash. Steam green beans until tender. Mix all ingredients together.

RECIPES FOR COMMON CONDITIONS 75

TURKEY, QUINOA, AND SPINACH BOWL

- 1 cup ground turkey, cooked: Lean protein source, high in vitamins and minerals
- 1 cup cooked quinoa: High in protein, gluten-free, and rich in essential amino acids
- 1 cup steamed spinach: High in vitamins A, C, and K, as well as iron and antioxidants
- 1 tbsp chia seeds: Omega-3 fatty acids and fiber for joint health

Cook ground turkey in a non-stick pan until fully cooked. Prepare quinoa according to package instructions. Steam spinach until wilted. Mix all ingredients together, adding chia seeds.

BEEF AND CHICKPEA STEW WITH PUMPKIN

- 1 cup lean ground beef, cooked: Protein source, rich in iron and B vitamins
- 1 cup cooked chickpeas: High in fiber, protein, and essential nutrients like folate and manganese
- 1 cup cooked, mashed pumpkin: High in fiber and a good source of vitamins A and C
- 1 tsp turmeric: Natural anti-inflammatory for joint support

Cook ground beef in a non-stick pan until fully cooked. Cook chickpeas according to package instructions. Cook pumpkin until tender, then mash. Mix all ingredients together, adding turmeric.

SALMON AND LENTIL MEDLEY

- 1 cup baked or steamed salmon, flaked: High in omega-3 fatty acids for healthy skin, coat, and joint support
- 1 cup cooked lentils: High in protein, fiber, and essential nutrients like iron and folate
- 1 cup steamed broccoli: Source of vitamins K, C, and A, as well as fiber and potassium

Bake or steam salmon until fully cooked, then flake. Cook lentils according to package instructions. Steam broccoli until tender. Mix all ingredients together.

TOFU AND SWEET POTATO BOWL

- 1 cup firm tofu, cubed and cooked: Plant-based protein, source of calcium for bone health
- 1 cup cooked sweet potatoes, cubed: High in fiber, beta-carotene, and vitamins B6 and C
- 1 cup steamed peas: Good source of vitamins A, K, and B, as well as fiber and protein

Cube and cook tofu in a non-stick pan until golden brown. Cook sweet potatoes until tender, then cube. Steam peas until tender. Mix all ingredients together.

RECIPES FOR COMMON CONDITIONS 77

LAMB AND BARLEY WITH CARROTS

- 1 cup ground lamb, cooked: High-quality protein, good source of essential vitamins and minerals
- 1 cup cooked barley: High in fiber and rich in essential nutrients like selenium and manganese
- 1 cup diced carrots, steamed: High in vitamin A for eye health and a good source of fiber
- 1 tsp ginger: Natural anti-inflammatory for joint support

Cook ground lamb in a non-stick pan until fully cooked. Prepare barley according to package instructions. Steam carrots until tender. Mix all ingredients together, adding ginger.

PORK AND BROWN RICE WITH GREEN BEANS

- 1 cup lean pork, cooked and diced: High-quality protein source, rich in B vitamins and minerals
- 1 cup cooked brown rice: High in fiber and essential nutrients like manganese and selenium
- 1 cup steamed green beans: Low in calories, source of vitamins A, C, and K
- 1 tbsp fish oil: Omega-3 fatty acids for joint health

Cook pork and dice into bite-sized pieces. Cook brown rice according to package instructions. Steam green beans until tender. Mix all ingredients together, adding fish oil.

EGG, COTTAGE CHEESE, AND RASPBERRY SCRAMBLE

- 2 large eggs, scrambled: High-quality protein source, rich in vitamins and minerals
- 1/2 cup cottage cheese: Calcium for bone health and a good source of protein
- 1/2 cup raspberries: Antioxidants for immune support
- 1 tbsp ground flaxseed: Omega-3 fatty acids for joint health

Scramble eggs in a non-stick pan. Mix all ingredients together, adding cottage cheese, raspberries, and flaxseed.

VENISON, SWEET POTATO, AND TURMERIC MASH

- 1 cup ground venison, cooked: High in protein, essential vitamins and minerals, and a novel protein source for allergy-prone dogs
- 1 cup cooked sweet potatoes, mashed: High in fiber, beta-carotene, and vitamins B6 and C
- 1 cup steamed kale: High in vitamins A, C, and K, as well as antioxidants and fiber
- 1 tsp turmeric: Natural anti-inflammatory for joint support

Cook ground venison in a non-stick pan until fully cooked. Cook sweet potatoes until tender, then mash. Steam kale until tender. Mix all ingredients together, adding turmeric.

CHAPTER 8
PUPPY RECIPES

Puppies are generally more active and require higher energy levels compared to adult dogs due to their growth and development and it means that puppies should be fed around 5-6% of their body weight per day.

The age at which a puppy is considered no longer a puppy can vary depending on the breed and individual development. Generally, small to medium-sized breeds are considered adults around 12 months of age, while larger breeds may take longer to reach adulthood, typically between 18 to 24 months. It's important to note that small and toy breeds may mature more quickly, reaching adulthood around 9 to 12 months of age.

It all means that puppies have unique nutritional requirements due to their rapid growth and development.

A 10 lb puppy needs around 900 calories a day (until they reach around 30 lbs) - this compares to older or senior dogs who only needs about 330 calories a day. Puppies also need more protein - they will need the higher end of the protein scale, anywhere between 20 and 30%.

It is also useful to note that once they hit their teenage years, although their energy requirement will fall, it will remain higher than it will as they grow into adulthood.

Growth and Development: Puppies go through a crucial stage of growth, where their bones, muscles, and organs develop rapidly. They require higher levels of protein, calcium, and other nutrients to support this growth. Recipes like Chicken and Sweet Potato Mash can provide the necessary protein and calcium for proper development.

Energy Needs: Puppies have higher energy requirements compared to adult dogs. They are active, playful, and constantly exploring their surroundings. The recipes designed for puppies, such as Beef and Rice Delight, contain a balance of protein, fat, and carbohydrates to provide the energy needed for their active lifestyles.

Strong Immune System: Puppies' immune systems are still developing, making them more susceptible to infections and diseases. The vitamins, minerals, and antioxidants found in recipes like Salmon and Quinoa Delight support a healthy immune system, helping puppies stay strong and protected.

Brain Development: Puppies' brains are rapidly growing and developing, and they need nutrients that support brain function and cognitive development. Omega-3 fatty acids, such as those found in Tuna and Chickpea Salad, are essential for brain health and can enhance learning and memory.

Dental Health: Puppies are in the early stages of dental development, and proper nutrition can contribute to healthy teeth and gums. Chewing on textured foods, as provided by recipes like Chicken Liver and Carrot Stir-Fry, can help promote good dental hygiene.

Healthy Skin and Coat: Puppies need essential fatty acids, such as omega-3 and omega-6, to maintain healthy skin and a shiny coat. Recipes like Duck and Green Bean Medley, which contain sources of these fatty acids, can help support skin health in puppies.

Digestive Health: Puppies have developing digestive systems that may be more sensitive. Recipes with easily digestible ingredients, such as Turkey and Brown Rice Bowl, can support healthy digestion and reduce the risk of digestive issues.

VITAMINS FOR PUPPIES

While the basic vitamins and minerals needed by puppies are similar to those needed by adult dogs, there are some key nutrients that may require special attention in their diet.

Calcium and phosphorus are crucial for proper bone and teeth development in puppies. The ratio of calcium to phosphorus is especially important, and excessive or insufficient levels of either mineral can have negative effects on skeletal health. Puppies generally require higher levels of calcium and phosphorus compared to adult dogs to support their rapid growth.

Vitamin D works in conjunction with calcium and phosphorus to promote proper bone formation and mineralization. It aids in the absorption and utilization of these minerals (and this is the same

82   HEALTHY HOMEMADE DOG FOOD COOKBOOK & GUIDE

for humans). It means that Vitamin D is important for supporting a puppy's skeletal development.

Vitamin A is essential for healthy vision, immune function, and cell growth. Because puppies are more susceptible to infections during the early stages of life they need adequate levels of vitamin A to support their immune system to protect their development.

Vitamin E is an antioxidant that helps protect cells from damage caused by free radicals. It supports the immune system and helps maintain healthy skin and coat in puppies.

B vitamins, including B1 (thiamine), B6 (pyridoxine), and B12 (cobalamin), play important roles in energy metabolism, brain development, and nerve function. Puppies need sufficient amounts of B vitamins to support their rapid growth and neurological development.

Iron is essential for the production of red blood cells and the transportation of oxygen throughout the body. Puppies require adequate iron for proper growth, development, and oxygenation of tissues.

Zinc is involved in various enzymatic reactions and is important for growth, immune function, and skin health. This, like the other vitamins, supports their development.

The specific nutrient requirements for puppies can vary based on factors such as breed, size, and individual needs.

The following puppy recipes are particularly good for puppies because they address their unique nutritional needs during the critical growth and development phase. Here's why:

High-Quality Protein: Puppies require higher amounts of protein for proper muscle development and tissue repair. The recipes include lean protein sources like chicken, beef, turkey, salmon, and lamb to meet these needs.

Essential Fatty Acids: Omega-3 fatty acids, found in fish like salmon and tuna, are crucial for brain development, vision health, and a shiny coat in puppies.

Balanced Nutrients: The recipes incorporate a variety of vegetables, grains, and fruits to provide a balanced array of vitamins, minerals, and antioxidants that support overall growth and development.

Digestive Health: Many recipes include ingredients like brown rice, quinoa, and pumpkin, which are gentle on the digestive system and provide dietary fiber to support healthy digestion.

Immune Support: The vitamins and antioxidants found in the recipes help strengthen the immune system of puppies, promoting their overall health and well-being.

Variety and Novel Protein Sources: Introducing a variety of proteins like chicken, beef, turkey, salmon, and lamb helps puppies develop diverse nutritional profiles and reduces the risk of developing allergies or sensitivities.

Remember that puppies have different nutrient requirements based on their breed, size, and individual needs. Don't forget to check with either your veterinarian or veterinary nutritionist to make sure that the recipes are suitable. They can also guide you on proper portion sizes, frequency of feeding, and any necessary modifications to the recipes for your particular puppy.

Most of the recipes that follow include chicken and beef are suitable for puppies 8 week and older although you want to wait until your puppy is 12 weeks or older before serving them salmon, fish, turkey or lamb.

CHICKEN AND SWEET POTATO MASH

Ingredients

- 2 lbs boneless, skinless chicken breasts (protein, vitamins B6, B12, niacin, selenium)
- 2 cups sweet potatoes, peeled and cubed (fiber, vitamins A, C, B6, potassium)
- 1 cup carrots, diced (fiber, vitamins A, K, potassium)
- 1 cup peas (fiber, vitamins A, C, K)
- 4 cups low-sodium chicken broth
- 1 tablespoon olive oil (fat)

Instructions

1. Heat olive oil in a large pot over medium heat.
2. Add chicken breasts and cook until browned on both sides.
3. Remove chicken from the pot and set aside.
4. In the same pot, add sweet potatoes, carrots, peas, and chicken broth.
5. Bring to a boil, then reduce heat and simmer until the vegetables are tender.
6. Meanwhile, shred the cooked chicken into bite-sized pieces.
7. Add the shredded chicken back to the pot and simmer for a few more minutes.
8. Cool then serve.

BEEF AND RICE DELIGHT

Ingredients

- 2 lbs lean ground beef (protein, iron, zinc, vitamins B12, B6)
- 2 cups spinach, chopped (fiber, vitamins A, C, K, iron)
- 1 cup carrots, grated (fiber, vitamins A, K, potassium)
- 1 cup green beans, chopped (fiber, vitamins C, K, manganese)
- 1 cup cooked brown rice
- 1 tablespoon coconut oil (fat)

Instructions

1. In a large skillet, cook the ground beef until browned and cooked through.
2. Drain excess fat from the skillet.
3. Add spinach, carrots, and green beans to the skillet and sauté until vegetables are tender.
4. Stir in the cooked brown rice and coconut oil.
5. Cook for a few more minutes to allow the flavors to blend and then cool.

SALMON AND QUINOA DELIGHT

Ingredients

- 1 lb salmon fillets, cooked and flaked (protein, omega-3 fatty acids, vitamins D, B3, B6, selenium)
- 2 cups cooked quinoa (protein, fiber, vitamins B1, B6, folate, iron)
- 1 cup peas (fiber, vitamins A, C, K)
- 1 cup carrots, diced (fiber, vitamins A, K, potassium)
- 1 cup broccoli florets (fiber, vitamins C, K, folate)
- 1 tablespoon fish oil (fat, omega-3 fatty acids)

Instructions

1. Cook the salmon fillets and flake them into bite-sized pieces.
2. In a large mixing bowl, combine the cooked quinoa, peas, carrots, and broccoli florets.
3. Add the flaked salmon to the bowl and mix well.
4. Drizzle fish oil over the mixture and stir to evenly distribute.
5. Serve the salmon and quinoa delight to your puppy after it has cooled.

TURKEY AND BROWN RICE BOWL

Ingredients

- 2 lbs lean ground turkey (protein, vitamins B3, B6, iron, selenium)
- 2 cups sweet potatoes, peeled and cubed (fiber, vitamins A, C, B6, potassium)
- 1 cup green beans, chopped (fiber, vitamins C, K, manganese)
- 1 cup peas (fiber, vitamins A, C, K)
- 1 cup cooked brown rice (fiber, vitamins B1, B3, iron, magnesium)
- 1 tablespoon olive oil (fat)

Instructions

1. In a large skillet, cook the ground turkey until browned and cooked through.
2. Drain excess fat from the skillet.
3. Add sweet potatoes, green beans, and peas to the skillet and sauté until vegetables are tender.
4. Stir in the cooked brown rice and olive oil.
5. Cook for a few more minutes so that the flavors can blend.
6. Cool and serve.

LAMB AND VEGETABLE STEW

Ingredients

- 3 lbs lamb shoulder, cubed (protein, vitamins B12, zinc, iron)
- 2 cups carrots, diced (fiber, vitamins A, K, potassium)
- 1 cup peas (fiber, vitamins A, C, K)
- 1 cup spinach, chopped (fiber, vitamins A, C, K, iron)
- 1 cup sweet potatoes, peeled and cubed (fiber, vitamins A, C, B6, potassium)
- 1 tablespoon olive oil (fat)

Instructions

1. Heat olive oil in a large pot over medium heat.
2. Add lamb shoulder cubes and cook until browned on all sides.
3. Remove lamb from the pot and set aside.
4. In the same pot, add carrots, peas, spinach, and sweet potatoes.
5. Pour enough water or low-sodium broth to cover the vegetables.
6. Bring to a boil, then reduce heat and simmer until the vegetables are tender.
7. Meanwhile, shred the cooked lamb into bite-sized pieces.
8. Add the shredded lamb back to the pot and simmer for a few more minutes.
9. Cool then store or serve.

TUNA AND CHICKPEA SALAD

Ingredients

1. 2 cups canned tuna, drained (protein, omega-3 fatty acids, vitamins D, B3, B6)
2. 2 cups cooked chickpeas (protein, fiber, vitamins B6, folate, iron)
3. 1 cup cucumber, diced (fiber, vitamins K, C)
4. 1 cup cherry tomatoes, halved (vitamins A, C, K)
5. 1/4 cup plain Greek yogurt (protein, calcium)
6. 2 tablespoons lemon juice (vitamin C)
7. 1 tablespoon olive oil (fat)
8. Fresh parsley, chopped (vitamins A, C, K)

Instructions

1. In a large mixing bowl, combine the tuna, cooked chickpeas, cucumber, and cherry tomatoes.
2. In a separate small bowl, whisk together the Greek yogurt, lemon juice, and olive oil to create the dressing.
3. Pour the dressing over the tuna and chickpea mixture and toss gently to coat.
4. Sprinkle fresh parsley on top for added flavor and nutrition.
5. Serve the tuna and chickpea salad to your puppy after it has cooled.

PORK AND PUMPKIN MASH

Ingredients

- 2 lbs lean ground pork (protein, vitamins B1, B6, iron, selenium)
- 2 cups pumpkin puree (fiber, vitamins A, C, E, potassium)
- 1 cup carrots, grated (fiber, vitamins A, K, potassium)
- 1 cup green peas (fiber, vitamins A, C, K)
- 1 cup cooked quinoa (protein, fiber, vitamins B1, B6, folate, iron)
- 1 tablespoon coconut oil (fat)

Instructions

1. In a large skillet, cook the ground pork until browned and cooked through.
2. Drain excess fat from the skillet.
3. Add pumpkin puree, grated carrots, and green peas to the skillet and cook until heated through.
4. Stir in the cooked quinoa and coconut oil.
5. Cook for a few more minutes to let everything blend together before cooling.

CHICKEN LIVER AND CARROT STIR-FRY

Ingredients

- 1 lb chicken livers, sliced (protein, vitamins A, B12, D, iron)
- 2 cups carrots, julienned (fiber, vitamins A, K, potassium)
- 1 cup broccoli florets (fiber, vitamins C, K, folate)
- 1 cup bell peppers, sliced (vitamin C, antioxidants)
- 1 tablespoon olive oil (fat)
- 1 teaspoon turmeric powder (anti-inflammatory properties)

Instructions

1. Heat olive oil in a large skillet or wok over medium heat.
2. Add chicken livers and cook until browned on all sides.
3. Remove chicken livers from the skillet and set aside.
4. In the same skillet, add carrots, broccoli, and bell peppers.
5. Stir-fry the vegetables until crisp-tender.
6. Add the cooked chicken livers back to the skillet.
7. Sprinkle turmeric powder over the mixture and stir well to coat.
8. Cook for a few more minutes until everything is heated through. Cool then serve.

DUCK AND GREEN BEAN MEDLEY

Ingredients

- 2 lbs duck breast, cooked and thinly sliced (protein, vitamins A, B5, B12, iron)
- 2 cups green beans, trimmed and halved (fiber, vitamins C, K, manganese)
- 1 cup butternut squash, cubed (fiber, vitamins A, C, E, potassium)
- 1 cup blueberries (antioxidants, vitamins C, K)
- 1 tablespoon coconut oil (fat)

Instructions

1. In a large skillet, cook the duck breast until fully cooked and slice it into thin strips.
2. In the same skillet, add green beans and butternut squash.
3. Sauté the vegetables until they are tender-crisp.
4. Add the sliced duck breast and blueberries to the skillet.
5. Drizzle coconut oil over the mixture and stir well to combine.
6. Cook for a few more minutes until everything is heated through.
7. Allow the duck and green bean medley to cool before serving it to your puppy.

QUINOA AND BLACK BEAN FIESTA

Ingredients

- 2 cups cooked quinoa (protein, fiber, vitamins B1, B6, folate, iron)
- 1 cup black beans, cooked (protein, fiber, vitamins B1, B6, iron)
- 1 cup bell peppers, diced (vitamin C, antioxidants)
- 1 cup tomatoes, diced (vitamin C, antioxidants)
- 1/4 cup fresh cilantro, chopped (vitamins A, C, K)
- 2 tablespoons lime juice (vitamin C)
- 1 tablespoon olive oil (fat)

Instructions

1. In a large mixing bowl, combine cooked quinoa, black beans, bell peppers, and tomatoes.
2. Add fresh cilantro to the bowl and mix well.
3. Drizzle lime juice and olive oil over the mixture and toss gently to coat.
4. Serve the quinoa and black bean fiesta to your puppy after it has cooled.

These recipes should provide a variety of nutritious meals for your puppy. Remember to adjust portion sizes according to your puppy's age, size, and activity level.

CHAPTER 9
RECIPES FOR SENIOR DOGS

Senior dogs have unique nutritional needs compared to adult dogs, as their bodies undergo various changes with age. While the basic vitamins and minerals needed are similar, there are some key nutrients that may require special attention. The following are examples of some of the reasons why senior dogs can require specific support.

Although senior dogs need less calories a day (only around 330 for an average 33 lb dog) they often also need more protein - with the proportion rising from 20-30% to as much as 50%. I would highly recommend talking to your veterinarian or pet nutritionist to get this balance right for your own particular senior dog - its not always the right thing to increase protein intake to too high a level and may senior dogs might have underlying conditions.

Joint Health: As dogs age, their joints may become stiffer and less flexible, leading to conditions like arthritis. Ingredients such as omega-3 fatty acids, found in recipes like Salmon and Quinoa Delight, help reduce inflammation and support joint health.

Muscle Maintenance: Senior dogs may experience muscle loss or decreased muscle mass. Adequate protein intake, provided by recipes like Beef and Vegetable Mash, helps maintain muscle strength and function.

Digestive Health: Older dogs may have slower digestion and a higher risk of gastrointestinal issues. Recipes with easily digestible proteins and added fiber, such as Chicken and Sweet Potato Stew, can support digestive health and regular bowel movements.

Immune System Support: Ageing can weaken the immune system, making senior dogs more susceptible to infections and diseases. Recipes containing vitamins A, C, and E, such as Lamb and Vegetable Stew, provide antioxidants and support immune system function.

Cognitive Health: Some senior dogs may experience cognitive decline, similar to Alzheimer's disease in humans. Ingredients like omega-3 fatty acids and antioxidants found in Tuna and Chickpea Salad can support brain health and cognitive function.

Dental Health: Dental issues, such as tooth decay and gum disease, become more common in senior dogs. Chewing on harder textures, like those found in Turkey and Brown Rice Bowl, can help promote dental health and reduce plaque buildup.

Weight Management: Senior dogs often have reduced activity levels, which can lead to weight gain. Recipes with balanced protein and fat levels, such as Bison and Spinach Saute, can help maintain a healthy weight and prevent obesity-related issues.

VITAMINS AND MINERALS

Vitamin C: As dogs age, their immune system may become weaker. Vitamin C acts as an antioxidant and supports immune function. It helps protect against oxidative stress and supports overall health. While dogs can produce their own vitamin C, senior dogs may benefit from additional supplementation or increased dietary intake.

Vitamin E is also an antioxidant that helps protect cells from damage caused by free radicals. It plays a role in supporting immune function and maintaining healthy skin and coat.

B Vitamins: B vitamins, including B1 (thiamine), B6 (pyridoxine), and B12 (cobalamin), are important for senior dogs. These vitamins are involved in energy metabolism, brain function, and nerve health. Ensuring an adequate intake of B vitamins can help support energy levels and cognitive function.

Vitamin D is essential for calcium absorption and bone health which means that it an important support to control bone density and prevent issues like osteoporosis or fractures (this is the same for women during and after the menopause). Older dogs can also have reduced ability to synthesize vitamin D from sunlight due to changes in their skin and metabolism.

Vitamin A plays a vital role in maintaining healthy vision, supporting immune function, and promoting healthy skin and coat. Including foods rich in vitamin A, such as carrots, sweet potatoes, or liver are particularly important for your older dog.

Vitamin B12: Senior dogs may have a reduced ability to absorb vitamin B12, which is important for nerve function, energy metabolism, and the production of red blood cells. Adequate vitamin B12 intake is essential for maintaining their overall health and vitality.

Coenzyme Q10 (CoQ10) is an antioxidant that helps support heart health and may have beneficial effects on cognitive function. Supplementing with CoQ10 can be beneficial for senior dogs, especially those with cardiac issues or cognitive decline.

Omega-3 Fatty Acids: Omega-3 fatty acids, such as EPA and DHA, have anti-inflammatory properties and can support joint health, cognitive function, and a healthy coat.

Glucosamine and Chondroitin: These compounds are essential for maintaining healthy joint function and supporting cartilage health. Senior dogs, especially those with arthritis or joint issues, may benefit from supplementation with glucosamine and chondroitin to promote mobility and reduce joint discomfort.

Minerals for Bone Health: Calcium, phosphorus, and magnesium remain important for senior dogs to support their bone health. However, the ratios and overall levels may need to be adjusted based on their individual needs and any specific health conditions.

The recipes below are specifically good for senior dogs because they consider their changing nutritional needs and health concern some of which are outlined below:

Reduced Calories: Senior dogs often have lower energy requirements due to decreased activity levels and metabolism. These recipes are designed to provide balanced nutrition while managing calorie intake to help maintain a healthy weight.

High-Quality Protein: They often require a higher protein content to support muscle maintenance and repair. The recipes

RECIPES FOR SENIOR DOGS

include lean protein sources such as chicken, turkey, beef, lamb, and fish to meet these needs.

Digestive Health: Many of the recipes incorporate easily digestible ingredients like rice, sweet potatoes, and vegetables to support digestive health and nutrient absorption in senior dogs.

Joint Support: Some recipes include ingredients rich in omega-3 fatty acids, such as salmon and tuna, which can help reduce inflammation and support joint health in senior dogs.

Antioxidant-Rich Ingredients: Senior dogs can benefit from antioxidants that help combat free radicals and support their immune system. The recipes include ingredients like vegetables and fruits, which provide vitamins A, C, and E, as well as other antioxidants.

Nutrient-Dense Ingredients: Senior dogs may have reduced nutrient absorption, so nutrient-dense ingredients are essential. These recipes include a variety of vitamins and minerals that help meet their nutritional requirements.

As you can see, I have selected recipes that address some of the general needs of our ageing pups, providing them the nutrition support that they may need to protect their overall health and well-being in their golden years.

Here are the 10 recipes, including the ingredients, nutritional information, and recipe instructions.

CHICKEN AND BROWN RICE MEDLEY

Ingredients

- 2 lbs boneless, skinless chicken breasts, cooked and shredded (protein, vitamins B6, B12, D, iron)
- 2 cups cooked brown rice (fiber, vitamins B1, B3, iron)
- 1 cup carrots, grated (fiber, vitamins A, K, potassium)
- 1 cup green beans, chopped (fiber, vitamins C, K, manganese)
- 1 cup pumpkin puree (fiber, vitamins A, C, E, potassium)
- 1 tablespoon fish oil (fat, omega-3 fatty acids)

Instructions

1. In a large mixing bowl, combine the shredded chicken, cooked brown rice, grated carrots, chopped green beans, and pumpkin puree.
2. Drizzle fish oil over the mixture and stir well to combine.
3. Serve the chicken and brown rice medley to your senior dog after it has cooled.

TURKEY AND SWEET POTATO STEW

Ingredients

- 2 lbs lean ground turkey (protein, vitamins B3, B6, iron, selenium)
- 2 cups sweet potatoes, peeled and cubed (fiber, vitamins A, C, B6, potassium)
- 1 cup peas (fiber, vitamins A, C, K)
- 1 cup green beans, chopped (fiber, vitamins C, K, manganese)
- 1 cup carrots, diced (fiber, vitamins A, K, potassium)
- 1 tablespoon coconut oil (fat)

Instructions

1. In a large skillet, cook the ground turkey until browned and cooked through.
2. Drain excess fat from the skillet.
3. Add sweet potatoes, peas, green beans, and carrots to the skillet and sauté until vegetables are tender.
4. Stir in the coconut oil
5. Cook for a few more minutes to let the ingredients blend.
6. Allow the turkey and sweet potato stew to cool then serve.

SALMON AND QUINOA DELIGHT

Ingredients

- 2 lbs salmon fillets, cooked and flaked (protein, omega-3 fatty acids, vitamins D, B3, B6, selenium)
- 2 cups cooked quinoa (protein, fiber, vitamins B1, B6, folate, iron)
- 1 cup peas (fiber, vitamins A, C, K)
- 1 cup carrots, diced (fiber, vitamins A, K, potassium)
- 1 cup broccoli florets (fiber, vitamins C, K, folate)
- 1 tablespoon fish oil (fat, omega-3 fatty acids)

Instructions

1. Cook the salmon fillets and flake them into bite-sized pieces.
2. In a large mixing bowl, combine the cooked quinoa, peas, carrots, and broccoli florets.
3. Add the flaked salmon to the bowl and mix well.
4. Drizzle fish oil over the mixture and stir to evenly distribute.
5. Serve the salmon and quinoa delight when cool.

RECIPES FOR SENIOR DOGS

BEEF AND VEGETABLE STIR-FRY

Ingredients

- 2 lbs lean beef, thinly sliced (protein, vitamins B6, B12, iron, zinc)
- 2 cups mixed vegetables (carrots, broccoli, green beans, bell peppers), chopped (fiber, vitamins A, C, K)
- 1 cup brown rice, cooked (fiber, vitamins B1, B3, iron)
- 2 tablespoons low-sodium soy sauce (sodium)
- 1 tablespoon olive oil (fat)

Instructions

1. In a large skillet or wok, heat olive oil over medium-high heat.
2. Add the sliced beef and stir-fry until browned and cooked to your desired level
3. Remove the beef from the skillet and set aside.
4. In the same skillet, add the mixed vegetables and stir-fry until crisp-tender.
5. Return the cooked beef to the skillet and add the cooked brown rice.
6. Drizzle the low-sodium soy sauce over the mixture and toss well to combine.
7. Cook for a few more minutes until everything is heated through.
8. Cool before serving.

LAMB AND SWEET POTATO CASSEROLE

Ingredients

- 2 lbs lean ground lamb (protein, vitamins B6, B12, iron, zinc)
- 2 cups sweet potatoes, peeled and cubed (fiber, vitamins A, C, B6, potassium)
- 1 cup green peas (fiber, vitamins A, C, K)
- 1 cup carrots, diced (fiber, vitamins A, K, potassium)
- 1 cup spinach, chopped (fiber, vitamins A, C, K, iron)
- 1 tablespoon coconut oil (fat)

Instructions

1. In a large skillet, cook the ground lamb until browned and cooked through.
2. Drain excess fat from the skillet.
3. Add sweet potatoes, green peas, carrots, and spinach to the skillet and sauté until vegetables are tender.
4. Stir in the coconut oil.
5. Cook for a few more minutes to let the flavors to meld together.
6. As always, cool then store or serve.

CHICKEN LIVER AND QUINOA PILAF

Ingredients

- 2 lbs chicken livers, sliced (protein, vitamins A, B12, D, iron)
- 2 cups cooked quinoa (protein, fiber, vitamins B1, B6, folate, iron)
- 1 cup green beans, chopped (fiber, vitamins C, K, manganese)
- 1 cup carrots, grated (fiber, vitamins A, K, potassium)
- 1 cup bell peppers, diced (vitamin C, antioxidants)
- 1 tablespoon olive oil (fat)

Instructions

1. In a large skillet, cook the sliced chicken livers until browned on all sides.
2. Remove the chicken livers from the skillet and set aside.
3. In the same skillet, add green beans, grated carrots, and diced bell peppers.
4. Sauté the vegetables until tender-crisp.
5. Add the cooked quinoa and cooked chicken livers back to the skillet.
6. Drizzle olive oil over the mixture and stir well to combine.
7. Cook for a few more minutes until everything is heated through.
8. Cool before serving.

TURKEY AND VEGETABLE STEW

Ingredients

- 2 lbs lean ground turkey (protein, vitamins B3, B6, iron, selenium)
- 2 cups mixed vegetables (carrots, peas, green beans, zucchini), chopped (fiber, vitamins A, C, K)
- 1 cup sweet potatoes, peeled and cubed (fiber, vitamins A, C, B6, potassium)
- 1 cup tomatoes, diced (vitamin C, antioxidants)
- 1 tablespoon coconut oil (fat)

Instructions

1. In a large pot or Dutch oven, cook the ground turkey until browned and cooked through.
2. Drain excess fat from the pot.
3. Add mixed vegetables, sweet potatoes, and tomatoes to the pot.
4. Stir in the coconut oil.
5. Add enough water or low-sodium broth to cover the ingredients.
6. Bring the stew to a boil, then reduce the heat and simmer for about 20 minutes or until the vegetables are tender.
7. Allow the turkey and vegetable stew to cool before serving it to your senior dog.

FISH AND POTATO BAKE

Ingredients

- 2 lbs white fish fillets (such as cod or haddock), cut into chunks (protein, omega-3 fatty acids, vitamins B6, B12, D, selenium)
- 2 cups potatoes, peeled and cubed (fiber, vitamins C, B6, potassium)
- 1 cup green peas (fiber, vitamins A, C, K)
- 1 cup carrots, diced (fiber, vitamins A, K, potassium)
- 1 cup spinach, chopped (fiber, vitamins A, C, K, iron)
- 1 tablespoon olive oil (fat)

Instructions

1. Preheat the oven to 375°F (190°C).
2. In a large baking dish, combine the fish chunks, potatoes, green peas, carrots, and spinach.
3. Drizzle olive oil over the mixture and toss gently to coat.
4. Cover the baking dish with foil and bake for about 25 minutes or until the fish is cooked through and the vegetables are tender.
5. Give it time to cool before serving to your senior dog.

PORK AND VEGETABLE STIR-FRY

Ingredients

2 lbs lean pork, thinly sliced (protein, vitamins B6, B12, iron, zinc)

2 cups mixed vegetables (carrots, bell peppers, snap peas, broccoli), sliced (fiber, vitamins A, C, K)

1 cup brown rice, cooked (fiber, vitamins B1, B3, iron)

2 tablespoons low-sodium soy sauce (sodium)

1 tablespoon olive oil (fat)

Instructions

In a large skillet or wok, heat olive oil over medium-high heat.

Add the sliced pork and stir-fry until browned and cooked through.

Remove the pork from the skillet and set aside.

In the same skillet, add the mixed vegetables and stir-fry until crisp-tender.

Return the cooked pork to the skillet and add the cooked brown rice.

Drizzle the low-sodium soy sauce over the mixture and toss well to combine.

Cook for a few more minutes until everything is heated through.

As always, cool before serving to your senior dog.

LAMB AND LENTIL STEW

Ingredients

- 2 lbs lean lamb, cubed (protein, vitamins B6, B12, iron, zinc)
- 2 cups lentils, cooked (protein, fiber, vitamins B1, B6, iron)
- 1 cup carrots, diced (fiber, vitamins A, K, potassium)
- 1 cup peas (fiber, vitamins A, C, K)
- 1 cup butternut squash, cubed (fiber, vitamins A, C, E, potassium)
- 1 tablespoon coconut oil (fat)

Instructions

1. In a large pot or Dutch oven, brown the lamb cubes on all sides.
2. Remove the lamb from the pot and set aside.
3. Add carrots, peas, and butternut squash to the pot and sauté until slightly softened.
4. Return the lamb to the pot and add the cooked lentils.
5. Stir in the coconut oil.
6. Bring the stew to a boil, then reduce the heat and simmer for about 1 hour or until the lamb is tender and the flavors have melded together.
7. Cool before storing or serving.

CHAPTER 10
DOG TREAT RECIPES

Dog treats are great fun to make, and they can save a great deal of money too!

I am going to start with my personal favorite - Liver Cake. I have written about it many times. If you are training a puppy right now then you will want to put this book down and go and make this cake!

LIVER CAKE

Ingredients

- 450 g Liver (lamb, ox or pig)
- 450 Wholemeal flour
- 3 Eggs
- Water

Instructions

Pre-heat the oven to 180 degrees (350F).

Add the eggs to a bowl and beat lightly. Add the same amount of water as eggs (you can always add more at the end so don't overdo the water at this stage). Add the flour.

Blend the liver then add it to the bowl with the flour, water, and eggs. Mix well. You need the consistency to be 'sticky' and not too runny - if its too thick add a little more water. Pop it in a cake baking tin.

Bake for for 30 – 45 minute minutes, cool, then you can cut into treat sized pieces or break a bit off as and when needed.

Here are a few more 10 easy-to-make healthy and tasty dog treats that you can make at home:

PEANUT BUTTER BANANA BITES

Ingredients

- 1 ripe banana, mashed
- 1/2 cup natural peanut butter (unsalted, no added sugar)
- 1 cup rolled oats

Instructions

1. Preheat oven to 350°F (175°C) and line a baking sheet with parchment paper.
2. In a mixing bowl, combine the mashed banana and peanut butter.
3. Gradually add the rolled oats to the mixture, stirring well to combine.
4. Drop spoonfuls of the mixture onto the prepared baking sheet.
5. Bake for 15-20 minutes or until the treats are golden brown and firm.
6. Allow time to cool.

Each treat contains approximately 40 calories.

CARROT AND APPLE BISCUITS

Ingredients

- 1 cup grated carrot
- 1 cup grated apple
- 2 cups whole wheat flour
- 1/4 cup unsweetened applesauce

Instructions

1. Preheat the oven to 350°F (175°C) and line a baking sheet with parchment paper.
2. In a large bowl, combine the grated carrot, grated apple, whole wheat flour, and unsweetened applesauce.
3. Mix well until the ingredients form a dough-like consistency.
4. Roll out the dough on a floured surface to about 1/4 inch thickness.
5. Use cookie cutters to cut out desired shapes and place them on the prepared baking sheet.
6. Bake for 25-30 minutes or until the biscuits are firm and lightly browned.
7. Make sure that the biscuits are completely cool before giving them to your dog. Store in an airtight container for up to two weeks.

Each biscuit contains approximately 50 calories.

SWEET POTATO CHEWS

Ingredients

- 2 large sweet potatoes

Instructions

1. Preheat the oven to 250°F (120°C) and line a baking sheet with parchment paper.
2. Wash and peel the sweet potatoes.
3. Cut the sweet potatoes into thin slices or strips, about 1/4 inch thick.
4. Place the sweet potato slices on the prepared baking sheet in a single layer.
5. Bake for 2-3 hours, flipping the slices halfway through, until they are dried and crispy.
6. Cool completely before store. They can be kept in an airtight container for up to two weeks.

Each sweet potato chew contains approximately 30 calories.

BLUEBERRY AND YOGURT FROZEN TREATS

Ingredients

- 1 cup plain Greek yogurt
- 1/2 cup fresh or frozen blueberries

Instructions

1. In a blender or food processor, combine the Greek yogurt and blueberries.
2. Blend until smooth and well mixed.
3. Pour the mixture into ice cube trays or silicone molds.
4. Place the trays or molds in the freezer and freeze until solid.
5. Once frozen, remove the treats from the trays or molds and store them in a freezer-safe container.
6. Serve the frozen treats as a refreshing snack on hot days.

Each treat contains approximately 20 calories.

SALMON AND SWEET POTATO BALLS

Ingredients

- 1 can wild-caught salmon, drained
- 1/2 cup cooked sweet potato, mashed
- 1/4 cup oat flour (you can make your own by grinding rolled oats in a blender)

Instructions

1. Preheat the oven to 350°F (175°C) and line a baking sheet with parchment paper.
2. In a mixing bowl, combine the drained salmon, mashed sweet potato, and oat flour.
3. Mix well until all the ingredients are evenly incorporated.
4. Roll the mixture into small balls, about the size of a tablespoon, and place them on the prepared baking sheet.
5. Bake for 15-20 minutes or until the balls are firm and lightly browned.
6. Allow the balls time to cool and you can store in an airtight container in the refrigerator for up to a week.

Each ball contains approximately 30 calories.

SPINACH AND CHEESE BISCUITS

Ingredients

- 2 cups whole wheat flour
- 1 cup fresh spinach, finely chopped
- 1/2 cup grated cheddar cheese
- 1/4 cup unsweetened applesauce
- 1/4 cup water

Instructions

1. Preheat the oven to 350°F (175°C) and line a baking sheet with parchment paper.
2. In a large bowl, combine the whole wheat flour, chopped spinach, grated cheddar cheese, applesauce, and water.
3. Mix well until a dough forms.
4. Roll out the dough on a floured surface to about 1/4 inch thickness.
5. Use cookie cutters to cut out desired shapes and place them on the prepared baking sheet.
6. Bake for 20-25 minutes or until the biscuits are firm and lightly browned.
7. Allow the biscuits to cool completely before serving. They can be stored in an airtight container for up to two weeks.

Each biscuit contains approximately 40 calories.

PUMPKIN AND OATMEAL COOKIES

Ingredients

- 1 cup canned pumpkin puree (not pumpkin pie filling)
- 1/4 cup unsweetened applesauce
- 2 cups rolled oats
- 1/4 teaspoon cinnamon

Instructions

1. Preheat the oven to 350°F (175°C) and line a baking sheet with parchment paper.
2. In a mixing bowl, combine the pumpkin puree, applesauce, rolled oats, and cinnamon.
3. Stir well until all the ingredients are thoroughly mixed.
4. Scoop out spoonfuls of the mixture and place them on the prepared baking sheet.
5. Flatten each spoonful with the back of a spoon to create a cookie shape.
6. Bake for 15-20 minutes or until the cookies are firm and lightly browned.
7. After cooling, store in an airtight container for up to two weeks

Each cookie contains approximately 50 calories.

APPLE AND CINNAMON BISCUITS

Ingredients

2 cups whole wheat flour

cup grated apple

1/4 cup unsweetened applesauce

1/4 teaspoon cinnamon

Instructions

1. Preheat the oven to 350°F (175°C) and line a baking sheet with parchment paper.
2. In a large bowl, combine the whole wheat flour, grated apple, applesauce, and cinnamon.
3. Mix well until a dough forms.
4. Roll out the dough on a floured surface to about 1/4 inch thickness.
5. Use cookie cutters to cut out shapes and place them on the baking sheet.
6. Bake for 20-25 minutes or until the biscuits are firm and lightly browned.
7. Allow the biscuits to cool completely before serving. Store in an airtight container for up to two weeks.

Each biscuit contains approximately 40 calories.

CARROT AND APPLE BISCUITS

Ingredients

- 1 cup grated carrots
- 1/2 cup grated apple
- 2 cups whole wheat flour
- 1/4 cup unsweetened applesauce

Instructions

1. Preheat the oven to 350°F (175°C) and line a baking sheet with parchment paper.
2. In a mixing bowl, combine the grated carrots, grated apple, whole wheat flour, and unsweetened applesauce. Mix well until a dough forms.
3. Roll out the dough on a floured surface to about 1/4-inch thickness.
4. Use cookie cutters to cut out desired shapes or simply cut the dough into small squares.
5. Place the biscuits on the prepared baking sheet.
6. Bake in the preheated oven for about 20-25 minutes until the biscuits are firm and lightly golden then cool and store or serve.

Each biscuit contains approximately 40 calories.

CHAPTER 11
FOODS TO AVOID

The following few pages will give you some main ingredients that may cause issues in certain dogs. I will start with the foods you need to avoid before moving onto to more general problems with some foods. These lists are not exhaustive but simply highlight the most common foods and problems.

FOODS TO AVOID

There are several foods that can be harmful or toxic to dogs and should be avoided. Here's a list of common foods that are unsafe for dogs:

Alcohol: under no circumstances give your dog alcohol. It can cause vomiting, diarrhea, difficulty breathing, tremors, disorientation, coma, and even death in dogs.

Chocolate contains theobromine and caffeine, which can be toxic to dogs and cause vomiting, diarrhea, rapid breathing, increased heart rate, seizures, and even death.

Grapes and raisins: The effect the toxins have is still not definitive, but it they can cause Kidney failure.

Onions and garlic: Contain compounds that can damage red blood cells, causing anemia and can irritate the bowel. Garlic is less toxic than onions but can still be harmful in large amounts.

Avocado: Contains persin, which can cause vomiting and diarrhea in dogs.

Nuts: Pecans, Almonds, Walnuts - these have the potential to not only cause vomiting but possible pancreatitis. Macadamia nuts can cause weakness, vomiting, tremors, and hyperthermia in dogs.Peanuts and popcorn tend to be okay.

Alcohol: Can cause vomiting, diarrhea, difficulty breathing, tremors, disorientation, coma, and even death in dogs.

Caffeine: Found in coffee, tea, and some energy drinks, caffeine can cause rapid breathing, heart palpitations, muscle tremors, and even death in dogs.

Xylitol: This artificial sweetener is found in many sugar-free products like gum, candy, and baked goods. It can cause a rapid release of insulin in dogs, leading to hypoglycemia, seizures, and even death.

Raw yeast dough: Can expand in a dog's stomach, leading to bloating and potential life-threatening twisting of the stomach. Additionally, the fermentation of the dough can produce alcohol, leading to alcohol toxicity.

FOODS TO AVOID

Bones, especially cooked bones: Can splinter and cause obstructions or lacerations in a dog's digestive system.

Fatty and greasy foods: Can cause pancreatitis, which is inflammation of the pancreas, leading to severe vomiting, diarrhea, and abdominal pain.

Fruit pits and seeds: Some fruit pits and seeds (such as apple seeds, cherry pits, and peach pits) contain cyanide, which is poisonous to dogs.

Hops are used in the process of brewing beer. If you are a homebrew enthusiast, then you must keep hops out of the reach of your dog. Signs to look out for are increased breathing, a racing heart rate, and vomiting. In severe cases, death can occur.

This is not an exhaustive list, so always check if a food is safe before giving it to your dog, and remember that each dog will be different. For example I have one dog who is immediately sick if she eats any shellfish (specifically prawns) while her son is fine with it. Generally speaking I try to avoid all shellfish.

OTHER FOODS THAT CAN CAUSE PROBLEMS

Dairy products (e.g. milk, cream, cottage cheese): Some dogs may be lactose intolerant, which can lead to digestive issues like diarrhea, gas, or bloating. Observe your dog for any signs of intolerance when introducing dairy products. You can use alternatives if it's needed.

Legumes (e.g., lentils, chickpeas, and peas): Legumes can cause gas and bloating in some dogs. Additionally, the FDA has investigated a potential link between grain-free diets high in legumes and a type of heart disease called dilated cardiomyopathy (DCM) in dogs. While the connection is not fully understood, it's essential to be cautious when feeding legumes to your dog.

While **tofu** is generally considered safe for dogs, some dogs may be sensitive to soy products. If you notice any adverse reactions, consider using alternative protein sources.

Grains (e.g., barley, oatmeal, brown rice, and quinoa): While these grains are typically safe for dogs, some dogs may have sensitivities or allergies to specific grains (like one of my own dogs). If your dog has a grain allergy, and you are using dry grain-free kibble then check the carbohydrate content as well as other vitamins and consider using alternative sources like sweet potatoes or other grain-free options. I cover grain-free in more detail and provide recipes in Common Conditions chapter.

Brown rice versus white rice

You will noticed that brown rice mentioned in the recipes rather than 'white' rice. This is because brown rice is a fiber superstar and has more dietary fiber than white rice, which is great for keeping our pups' digestion in check and their bowel movements healthy. Plus, the extra fiber makes their bellies feel full and satisfied after meals, helping to keep their weight in balance.

Now, let's talk nutrients. Unlike white rice, brown rice keeps its nutrient-rich bran and germ layers during processing. This means it's packed with vitamins, minerals, and antioxidants, such as B vitamins, iron, manganese, magnesium, and selenium. All of these nutrients work together to keep our dogs healthy and happy!

And last but not least, brown rice has a lower glycemic index compared to white rice. This means it won't send our dogs' blood sugar levels through the roof, which can be especially important for pups prone to diabetes or obesity.

Of course, if your dog is a fan of white rice or has a sensitive stomach, white rice can still work for them and may be better. It's easy to digest, can help 'bind' and has a mild taste. But overall, brown rice is a top choice for providing our furry friends with the essential nutrients they need.

It's now time to start looking at some recipes as we build our knowledge of the content of our dog food. Bear in mind as you reading that much of this applies to humans too!

CHAPTER 12
CONCLUSION

hope you have enjoyed the book and that it has inspired you to try making your own dog food. I love it - but not as much as my dogs love eating it!

In the preceding pages we've delved into the world of homemade dog food, providing you with nutritious recipes and valuable insights into canine nutrition. By embracing homemade meals, you can take control of your dog's diet, ensuring they receive the best possible nutrition for optimal health and vitality.

Remember, the key to a successful homemade dog food journey is balance. Balancing proteins, fats, and carbohydrates, along with essential vitamins and minerals, is crucial for meeting your dog's nutritional needs. By offering a variety of protein sources, such as chicken, turkey, fish, and lean meats, you can provide a diverse mix of amino acids necessary for muscle growth, immune function, and overall well-being.

CONCLUSION

Don't forget the importance of high-quality carbohydrates like brown rice, quinoa, and sweet potatoes. These complex carbohydrates provide energy, fiber, and essential vitamins to support your dog's daily activities and digestive health.

Incorporating healthy fats, such as fish oil and flaxseed, helps promote a shiny coat, supports brain function, and provides important omega-3 fatty acids for heart health.

While our recipes offer a great starting point, it's essential to tailor your dog's diet to their specific needs. Factors such as age, weight, activity level, and any existing health conditions should be taken into account. Consulting with a veterinarian who understands your dog's unique requirements can provide valuable guidance and ensure that the homemade meals you prepare are truly customized for their optimal health.

Finally, regular monitoring of your dog's health and weight is crucial. Adjustments may be necessary to meet their changing nutritional needs over time. Keeping an open line of communication with your veterinarian will help you make informed decisions and maintain your dog's well-being.

I hope you it has provided you with the knowledge to embark on a journey of creating delicious and nutritious homemade meals for your furry friend. By investing your time and love into their diet, you are nurturing their overall health and happiness. Remember, the bond you share with your dog goes beyond food, but providing them with a wholesome diet is one way to demonstrate your dedication to their well-being.

With the information and recipes provided in this book, you are now ready to embark on a wonderful and fulfilling adventure of preparing homemade dog food. Your four-legged companion will be grateful for the tasty and nutritious meals that nourish their body, mind, and spirit. Here's to many wagging tails and a lifetime of good health together!

CHAPTER 13
FOOD PROTEINS AND CALORIC SUMMARY

The amount of protein and calories will depend on the cut of mean or fish, how the animal was reared and fed as well as how it is cooked. The following shows indicative levels of both.

MEAT

Chicken (no skin): 100 grams of chicken contains 25-30 grams of protein and around 100-120 calories. The skin is high in fat and if you include skin then you need to add quite a few calories - maybe as much as 20-50!

Lean ground beef (90% lean, 10% fat) contains around 20-25 grams of protein per 100 grams and 80-100 calories

Lamb: on average lamb 25-27 grams of protein per 100 grams and 100- 110 calories

Duck: around 25 grams of protein per 100 grams and 100-110 calories.

Pork: 25 grams of protein per 100 grams. Like other meat the cut makes a difference. Tenderloin or loin chops, contain around 100-150 calories per 100 grams while pork belly or ribs can reach 250-300 calories per 100 grams.

Turkey: 25-30 grams of protein per 100 grams.The calories can range from 100 all the way to 200 depending on how its cooked, if the skin is included and the cut of the meat. Aim for breast without skin.

Venison: 25-30 grams of protein per 100 grams and 100 to 120 but can be higher.

Bison: 25-30 grams of protein in 100 grams with calories of 100 to 120 or more.

FISH

Sardines: around 20-25 grams of protein per 100 grams and 150-200 calories. This is higher than the average protein to calorie count because of the healthy fats that sardines contain (and fats have a higher caloric conversion)

Salmon 100 grams contains around 25 grams of protein, and 200-250 calories. It is has a higher calorific value because it also contains lots of healthy fats.

Tuna, has a high protein content at around 25-30 grams per 100 grams of cooked meat. Calories are 120-150.

Whitefish (such as cod or haddock): 18-20 grams of protein per 100 grams and around 80-100 calories.

CHAPTER 14
MEASURING VITAMINS AND MINERALS

MEASUREMENTS AND AMOUNTS

t is always useful to have some awareness of how vitamins and minerals are measured. It can not only help you plan your own menu for your pup but it can help you understand some of the labelling on any bought dog food products.

The measurements that you will see are mg/day, IU/day, and mcg/day. So what are they?

A **mg/day** is simply milligrams per day and a milligram (mg) is one-thousandth of a gram.

An **IU/day** is the measurement of International Units per day; used to express the potency or biological activity of specific vitamins and hormones.

Finally **mcg/day** is micrograms per day; a microgram (mcg or µg) is one-millionth of a gram.

You usually convert IU/day to mg or mcg and, annoyingly, not all vitamins are created equal.

For example, with Vitamin D, 1 IU equals 0.025 mcg. To add 200 IU of Vitamin D to dog food, you would convert the IU to micrograms (200 IU * 0.025 mcg/IU = 5 mcg of Vitamin D) and use a sensitive digital scale to measure the required amount before mixing it thoroughly into the food.

Assuming an average dog weight of 33 pounds (15 kg), the following ranges of maximum and minimum intake serve as general guidelines and I have included a reminder of what each is good for. Remember, these are general guidelines,

Vitamin A

• Minimum: 1,125 IU/day

• Maximum: 6,750 IU/day

B Vitamins

• B1 (Thiamine): Min 0.56 mg/day

• B2 (Riboflavin): Min 1.3 mg/day

• B3 (Niacin): Min 4.5 mg/day, Max 67.5 mg/day

• B5 (Pantothenic Acid): Min 2.25 mg/day

• B6 (Pyridoxine): Min 0.23 mg/day

• B7 (Biotin): Min 22.5 mcg/day

• B9 (Folic Acid): Min 45 mcg/day

• B12 (Cobalamin): Min 4.5 mcg/day

MEASURING VITAMINS AND MINERALS

Vitamin C

- Minimum: 11.25 mg/day
- Maximum: 675 mg/day

Vitamin D

- Minimum: 225 IU/day
- Maximum: 900 IU/day

Vitamin E

- Minimum: 11.25 IU/day
- Maximum: 337.5 IU/day

Vitamin K

- Minimum: 0.15 mg/day

Calcium

- Minimum: 0.75 g/day
- Maximum: 3 g/day

Phosphorus

- Minimum: 0.6 g/day
- Maximum: 2.4 g/day

Magnesium

- Minimum: 112.5 mg/day

Potassium

- Minimum: 450 mg/day

Sodium

- Minimum: 150 mg/day

Chloride

- Minimum: 225 mg/day

Iron

- Minimum: 3.6 mg/day
- Maximum: 54 mg/day

Copper

- Minimum: 0.9 mg/day
- Maximum: 13.5 mg/day

Zinc

- Minimum: 6.75 mg/day
- Maximum: 50.4 mg/day

MEASURING VITAMINS AND MINERALS

Manganese

- Minimum: 0.9 mg/day

- Maximum: 13.5 mg/day

Selenium

- Minimum: 36 mcg/day

- Maximum: 540 mcg/day

Here are the conversions for some common vitamins from International Units (IU) to micrograms (mcg) or milligrams (mg). Please note that not all vitamins use IU as a measurement; for many, the standard unit is already in mg or mcg.

Vitamin A (retinol): 1 IU = 0.3 mcg
To convert from IU to mcg, multiply the IU value by 0.3.

Vitamin D (cholecalciferol): 1 IU = 0.025 mcg
To convert from IU to mcg, multiply the IU value by 0.025.

Vitamin E (α-tocopherol): 1 IU = 0.67 mg or 1 mg = 1.49 IU
To convert from IU to mg, multiply the IU value by 0.67.
To convert from mg to IU, multiply the mg value by 1.49.

The B vitamins and vitamin K are not typically measured in IU; their standard units are already in micrograms (mcg) or milligrams (mg).

For minerals, the standard units are also in micrograms (mcg) or milligrams (mg), and there is no need for conversion to IU.

Magnesium

Maximum: There isn't a well-defined maximum for magnesium. However, excessive magnesium intake can cause digestive issues and may interfere with the absorption of other minerals.

Potassium

Maximum: Like magnesium, there isn't a specific maximum for potassium. Excessive potassium intake is rare and usually related to an underlying medical condition rather than dietary intake. Consult your veterinarian to determine the appropriate potassium levels for your dog.

Sodium

Maximum: 600 mg/day. Excessive sodium intake can lead to health issues like high blood pressure and heart disease. Always provide fresh water for your dog, especially if their sodium intake is higher than usual.

Chloride

Maximum: The maximum for chloride is also not well-defined. Too much chloride can disrupt your dog's fluid balance and may cause health problems.

CHAPTER 15
VITAMINS AND MINERALS DIARY

Use this to add information as you discover and test out your recipes. Add-in the information on the ingredients that you are using and highlight the ones your pooch loves the best,

I have started and provided some examples.

MEAT, FISH AND POULTRY

Chicken: Rich in protein for muscle maintenance and growth

Duck: High in protein, essential vitamins and minerals, and a novel protein source for allergy-prone dogs

Salmon: High in omega-3 fatty acids for healthy skin and coat

. . .

Lean ground beef: Protein source, rich in iron and B vitamins

Whitefish or sardines: Rich in omega-3 fatty acids, high-quality protein source

Turkey: Lean protein source, high in vitamins and minerals

Pork: Lean pork provides high-quality protein, contains vitamins B6, B12, iron, and zinc, which support overall health and immune function.

DAIRY

Eggs: High-quality protein source, rich in vitamins and minerals

Yogurt: Provides calcium and probiotics for digestion and bone health.

VEGETABLES AND FRUITS

Bell peppers: High in vitamin C and antioxidants

Broccoli: Source of vitamins K, C, and A, as well as fiber and potassium

Butternut squash: High in fiber, vitamins A and C, and potassium

Carrots: High in vitamin A for eye health and a good source of fiber

Cauliflower: Low in calories, high in fiber, and a good source of vitamins C and K

Green beans: Low in calories, source of vitamins A, C, and K

Pumpkin: High in fiber and a good source of vitamins A and C

Spinach: High in vitamins A, C, and K, as well as iron and antioxidants

. . .

VITAMINS AND MINERALS DIARY   141

Sweet potatoes: High in fiber, beta-carotene, and vitamins B6 and C

Zucchini: Low in calories, high in fiber and antioxidants

Spinach: Rich in vitamins A, C, and K, as well as minerals like iron, calcium, and potassium. These nutrients support immune function, bone health

Blueberries: high in antioxidants and vitamin C, promoting a healthy immune system

LEGUMES

Chickpeas: High in fiber, protein, and essential nutrients like folate and manganese

Lentils: High in protein, fiber, and essential nutrients like iron and folate

GRAINS

Brown rice is a gentle source of carbohydrates and fiber, aiding digestion and providing B vitamins and iron for energy production and overall well-being.

CHAPTER 16
SHOPPING LIST

Here's a simple shopping list for you to whip up nutritious homemade meals for your dog. These ingredients will help you cover the essential nutrients your pup needs to stay healthy and happy. Just add any others from the last few resources to help you plan you meals.

Chicken (Protein)

- This lean protein provides essential amino acids, vitamin B, and minerals like iron and zinc.
- About 1 to 1.5 cups per day, depending on your dog's size and activity level.

Brown Rice (Carbohydrates)

- A great source of complex carbs, fiber, and B vitamins for energy and digestion.
- About 1/2 to 1 cup per day

Spinach (Vegetables)

Packed with vitamins A, K, and C, iron, and antioxidants to support the immune system and overall health.

- Around 1/4 to 1/2 cup per day.

Sweet Potato (Vegetables)

- Provides vitamins A, C, and E, potassium, and fiber for digestion and immune health.
- About 1/2 to 1 cup per day, depending on your dog's size and activity level.

Fish Oil (Fats)

- Loaded with omega-3 fatty acids for a healthy coat, skin, and immune system.
- Around 1,000 mg per day for small dogs and up to 3,000 mg per day for larger dogs.

Egg (Protein)

A complete protein with essential amino acids, vitamins, and minerals like calcium, phosphorus, and selenium.

- A complete protein with essential amino acids, vitamins, and minerals like calcium, phosphorus, and selenium.
- One whole egg per day for small to medium-sized dogs or two eggs for larger dogs.

Calcium Supplement

146   HEALTHY HOMEMADE DOG FOOD COOKBOOK & GUIDE

You may not need to supplement calcium if your dog is getting his requirements in his food. A reminder that calcium is needed for strong bones, teeth, and proper muscle function.

- About 500-700 mg per day, depending on your dog's size.

Once again a reminder that, for those interested, I have included measurement information of these at the end of the book.

As we have already mentioned, possibly more than once, when it comes to feeding our furry friends, it's important to provide a balanced diet, and just like us humans, different dog breeds have different nutritional needs. Factors like age, activity level, and overall health also play a role, as well as any pre-existing conditions.

Like anything, some things are good for us and some things are bad for us. In the next chapter I take a look at what foods you need to avoid.

CHAPTER 17
MORE INFORMATION

More information

For more information on dog nutrition and specific recommendations, you can consult the following resources:

National Research Council. (2006). Nutrient Requirements of Dogs and Cats. The National Academies Press. https://doi.org/10.17226/10668

American Veterinary Medical Association. https://www.avma.org/events/national-pet-week#nutrition

The Association of American Feed Control Officials. Pet Food. https://www.aafco.org/Consumers/Pet-Food

National Academies Press, Nutrient Requirements of Dogs and Cats https://nap.nationalacademies.org/resource/10668/dog_nutrition_final_fix.pdf

RECOMMENDED DOG TRAINING COURSE

I just came across this fantastic (and free) online workshop on training your dog to become as well-behaved as a service dog.

I loved the workshop so much that I wanted to share it with you.

Check out the free workshop here

The workshop is designed to help "normal" dogs like yours have the same level of calmness, obedience and impulse control as service dogs.

It's being conducted by Dr. Alexa Diaz (one of the top service dog trainers in the U.S.) and Eric Presnall (host of the hit Animal Planet TV show "Who Let the Dogs Out").

Frankly, the techniques described in the workshop are fairly groundbreaking - I haven't seen anyone else talk of these techniques.

This is because it's the first time ever (at least that I know of) that anyone has revealed the techniques used by the service dog training industry to train service dogs.

And more importantly, how any "regular" dog owner can apply the same techniques to train their own dogs to become as well-trained as service dogs.

It's not a live workshop - rather, it's a pre-recorded workshop, which means that you can watch it at your convenience.

However, while the workshop is free, I am not sure whether it's going to be online for too long, so please check it out as soon as you can.

Here's the link again.

Or you can use this QR code.

MORE BOOKS FROM TWENTY DOGS PUBLISHING

www.amazon.com/dp/B09F1F7Z6W

www.amazon.co.uk/dp/B09F1F7Z6W

Complete Puppy Amazon Link US

MORE BOOKS FROM TWENTY DOGS PUBLISHING

www.amazon.com/dp/B09DMR77SD

www.amazon.co.uk/dp/B09DMR77SD

German Shepherd Training Guide Amazon Link US

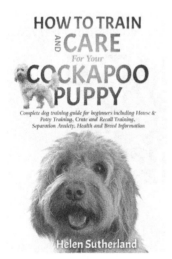

www.amazon.com/dp/1739983955

www.amazon.co.uk/dp/1739983955

Cockapoo Puppy Amazon Link US

MORE BOOKS FROM TWENTY DOGS PUBLISHING

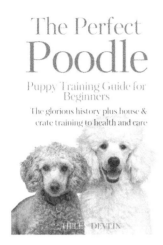

www.amazon.com/dp/B0B2TP5Z8K

www.amazon.co.uk/dp/B0B2TP5Z8K

The Perfect Poodle Amazon Link (US)

www.amazon.com/dp/B0C526728C

www.amazon.co.uk/dp/B0C526728C

Dog Behavior Problems and How To Solve Them (US)

LEAVE A REVIEW

If you enjoyed this book, I'd really appreciate it if you leave your honest feedback. You can do this by clicking the link to leave a review. I love hearing from my readers, and I personally read every single review.

Made in the USA
Las Vegas, NV
03 September 2023